P9-DXM-232

DATE DUE

MY 13 '94			
SE 16 '94			
OC 20 '95			
AP 5 '96 RENEW			
MY 7 '96			
MY 12 '97			
OC 1 '98			
86 22 00			
NO 23 '98			
AO 5 '00			
FE 12 '09			

DEMCO 38-296

PENGUIN BOOKS
SMART FOR LIFE

MICHAEL CHAFETZ, PH.D., is a research psychologist who currently works at a private neuropsychology clinic in the metropolitan New Orleans area. He has published numerous scholarly articles on the brain's control of behavior, and he has taught at Tulane University and the University of New Orleans. His previous book, *Nutrition and Neurotransmitters*, written for the field of behavioral neuroscience, is recognized for its synthesis of the neurobehavioral components of nutrition.

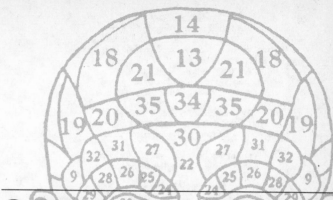

SMART FOR LIFE

How to Improve Your Brain Power at Any Age

Michael D. Chafetz, Ph.D.

PENGUIN BOOKS

Riverside Community College
Library
4800 Magnolia Avenue
Riverside, California 92506

JUN '93

PENGUIN BOOKS
Published by the Penguin Group
Viking Penguin, a division of Penguin Books USA Inc.,
375 Hudson Street, New York, New York 10014, U.S.A.
Penguin Books Ltd, 27 Wrights Lane,
London W8 5TZ, England
Penguin Books Australia Ltd, Ringwood,
Victoria, Australia
Penguin Books Canada Ltd, 10 Alcorn Avenue, Suite 300,
Toronto, Ontario, Canada M4V 3B2
Penguin Books (N.Z.) Ltd, 182–190 Wairau Road,
Auckland 10, New Zealand

Penguin Books Ltd, Registered Offices:
Harmondsworth, Middlesex, England

First published in Penguin Books 1992

1 3 5 7 9 10 8 6 4 2

Copyright © Michael D. Chafetz, 1992
All rights reserved

A NOTE TO THE READER: The ideas, procedures, and suggestions contained in this book, especially those pertaining to diet and nutrition, are not intended as a substitute for consulting with your physician. All matters regarding your health require medical supervision.

Grateful acknowledgment is made for permission to use the following copyrighted works:
Adaptation of figure of brain from *Psychology* by Henry Gleitman. By permission of W. W. Norton & Company, Inc. Copyright © 1981 by W. W. Norton & Company, Inc.
Selection from *More Games for the Super-intelligent* by James F. Fixx. Copyright © 1976 by James F. Fixx. Used by permission of Doubleday, a division of Bantam Doubleday Dell Publishing Group, Inc.
Figure of memory process from *Memory* by Elizabeth Loftus. By permission of the author.
Selection from *Your Memory: A User's Guide* by Alan D. Baddeley. Copyright © 1982 by Multimedia Publications, Ltd. Reprinted with permission of Macmillan Publishing Company.
Excerpt from *Catch 22* by Joseph Heller. Copyright © 1955, 1961, 1989 by Joseph Heller. Reprinted by permission of Simon & Schuster, Inc.

LIBRARY OF CONGRESS CATALOGING IN PUBLICATION DATA
Chafetz, Michael D.
Smart for life: how to improve your brain power at any age/
Michael D. Chafetz.
p.   cm.
Includes bibliographical references and index.
ISBN 0 14 01.3173 6
1. Intellect—Problems, exercises, etc.   2. Brain—Problems,
exercises, etc.   I. Title.
BF431.C393   1992
153.9—dc20   91–17799

Printed in the United States of America

Set in ITC Garamond Light with Univers Condensed 57
Designed by Beth Tondreau Design

Except in the United States of America, this book is sold subject to the condition that it shall not, by way of trade or otherwise, be lent, re-sold, hired out, or otherwise circulated without the publisher's prior consent in any form of binding or cover other than that in which it is published and without a similar condition including this condition being imposed on the subsequent purchaser.

FOR MY FATHER

It is not enough to have a good mind. The main thing is to use it well. —RENÉ DESCARTES

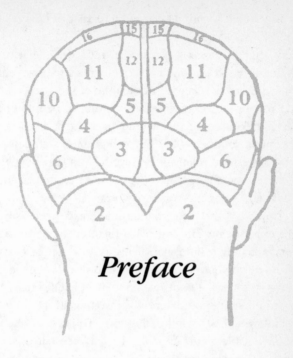

Preface

When I was a teenager, I had what I thought was a unique view of the world. I believed that whatever extraordinary accomplishments had been achieved in the past by a genius could, in subsequent years, be learned by any normal human being willing to commit sufficient time and energy. I based this view on what I had discovered about the history of human knowledge and what I felt about my own abilities to learn new things.

Like any other schoolboy flush with new knowledge, I was delighted (and felt superior) to think that what I was learning in high school had been taught in college and university courses only a generation before. Later, it occurred to me that this was how civilization progresses. At the time of a new discovery, few people understand it. As the discovered fact or theory ages, more and more people understand it until it becomes a regular college course, then a high school subject.

I saw this progression at work in my own intellectual life as well, when my best friend and I got together to attempt to understand Einstein's theories of relativity. At the time of Einstein's discovery in the early part of the century, only a handful of people understood what he was talking about. By the time my friend and I tried to master it, it was taught routinely—but not to high school students. No one we knew understood relativity, and we had no idea if we were capable of it, but my father loaned me a book that treated the subject in a simple and straightforward manner.

We slowly worked through the rudimentary math, as well as the "thought experiments" in which we pictured ourselves as unseen observers watching a little man living in his own box of a world, which from our point of view is moving upward. When the little man drops a tray, we saw the floor rise up to meet it. Of course, *he* would explain the phenomenon differently, invoking a force called gravity to "explain" why the tray fell to the floor. To illustrate the concepts further and enable us to appreciate what different observers see when they are moving relative to one another, we would also walk past each other and toss pillows as if they were beams of light traveling between us. When we finally arrived at Einstein's famous equation $E = MC^2$, we congratulated each other with a fervor suggesting we'd discovered it for the very first time. In a sense, we had, for each person's learning process is an original and creative act. Though I do not claim to have mastered relativity with my friend, I am certain from our initial experience that, had we stayed in the field, we could eventually have done so.

The exciting thing was that we had understood (with our normal minds) a genius's discovery. Because it did not take a genius to arrive at this understanding, I began to feel that a normal mind like my own could understand the products of any mind. All it took was a little push. (And a lot of hard work and tenacity.)

It was in graduate school that I began to understand the neurophysiology of why this is so—and how the "push" might be activated. When I began my studies of how the brain works, the neural sciences had only recently begun to refocus on nerve cells' amazing ability to change with experience. This plasticity included the growth of new nerve endings, formation of new connections, development of new proteins, and remodeling of the branches that receive incoming information.

The excitement among fellow biopsychologists and neuroscientists was infectious, and I was soon caught up in the idea that through our experiences we could remodel our brains and change the way we think. This view of the brain fit beautifully with my optimistic notion that the human mind can learn anything.

It also dawned on me that the opposite view—that we are limited to the minds we were born with—was based on an earlier concept. This view focused on absolute numbers of brain cells. Once our brain cells develop, they can only die off with age or destruction; we cannot make new brain cells in the same way we make new skin cells. Because we can never add new brain cells, this view said, we can never get smarter. Our intelligence is limited to the brains with which we are born.

A corollary to this idea is that individual intelligence is dependent on the number of brain cells we do have—the more the better. This idea has also been discredited, largely because the number of brain cells is in direct proportion to the size of the body they must control. (Otherwise, elephants would be quite a bit smarter than any one of us.) However, a relationship does exist between the *ratio* of brain to body size and the sophistication of the animal. The larger the brain with respect to the body it must control, the more sophisticated (behaviorally) the animal is. But these comparisons are mostly used for large classes of animals. For example, birds and mammals, with their larger brain to body ratios, are generally considered to be behaviorally more sophisticated than reptiles and amphibians. Also, primates generally have larger brain to body ratios than other mammals such as dogs or cats. But neuroscientists have yet to find any meaningful relationship between a person's brain/body ratio and his or her intelligence.

Now that our focus has shifted from number of brain cells to neural plasticity—the ability of brain cells to remodel and ramify their interconnections—we can easily challenge this view of a finite brain. At the very least, we now know that intelligence has to do with much more than mere brain size: People are not smart or stupid simply because they have more or fewer brain cells. You will be smarter if you work at remodeling the neural connections between cells (which happens if you are willing to learn from your experiences) and less smart if you allow them to wither with disuse.

We are beginning to acquire the technology that will allow us to understand the dynamics of plasticity, which might be defined as the ability of the brain to acquire more information as you challenge it at higher and higher levels. My fellow neuroscientists have developed scanning methods that let us (almost like voyeurs) glimpse the processes as they occur in the brains of conscious, thinking people. The principal technique—positron emission tomography (PET)—allows us to see the location and amount of glucose (the brain's main fuel) absorbed by neuronal circuits when they are activated by a challenge. Using this method, Harvard scientist Stephen Kosslyn has shown that when a person thinks about a visual image with his eyes closed, the brain's visual and spatial processing circuits work harder and absorb more glucose than when that visual image is actually seen. Thus, thinking and imagining presents the brain with more of a challenge than actually seeing an object. This stimulation of the brain's activity and ability to absorb more glucose also occurs in other neuronal circuits when different functions—language, memory, logic—are processed.

Whenever brain cells are activated by seeing, speaking, or solving problems, they begin to change. They take in more chemical energy and remodel nerve endings and receptors. They form new connections. In short, they become better at doing what they normally do. They become smarter.

If this sounds a little like exercise, the analogy is apt. The way to make yourself a smarter, more adaptable person is to "exercise" those brain areas that help you function in the world, just as you build up your biceps or quadriceps by exercising and using them in controlled and directed ways. By making those nerves utilize more energy and develop more receptors and enzymes your brain will help you function better. Moreover, in a similar way that the normal activity of walking might be regarded as physical exercise, everyday thinking can be structured as brain exercise.

There are mental techniques you can use to enhance your brain's inherent abilities. Though you may never be an Einstein or a Shakespeare, you can become better at solving problems, more fluent with language, more facile with logic, and you can learn to remember more detail. All you have to do is target your brain exercise to the neural circuits you want to improve, and let those circuits develop (like muscles) to become better at their normal functions.

The first step is to ready your brain for its exercise regimen. This is done by increasing your brain's general level of fitness—a concept closely related to increasing body fitness as a first step toward improving muscle power. Like body fitness, brain fitness is achieved by eating certain foods, avoiding certain drugs, preventing fatigue, and providing your brain with sleep, rewards, and the benefits of physical exercise. When your brain is fit and ready, then you can start on the brain exercises.

The wonderful thing about exercise, physical or mental, is that it doesn't matter what age you are when you start—improvement is always possible. If you are in a basic state of good health, your brain cells are capable of positive receptor, enzyme, and membrane changes at any age. But the sooner you start, the more time your brain will have to make these changes—and the longer you will benefit from them.

So, we should all keep the optimism of our adolescent days. The human mind has a capacity to learn in direct proportion to the challenges its owner is willing to meet, because the brain has physical and chemical properties that allow it to change for the better.

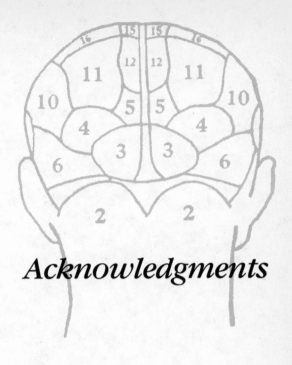

Acknowledgments

I am most grateful for the help and many acts of kindness from the following:
—Marjorie Esman, for her help in the trenches;
—Jim Corwin, Phil Best, and Cameron Camp, for their scientific imagination and general support;
—Jacques de Spoelberch, for the right stuff; and
—the professionals at Viking Penguin, for true quality.

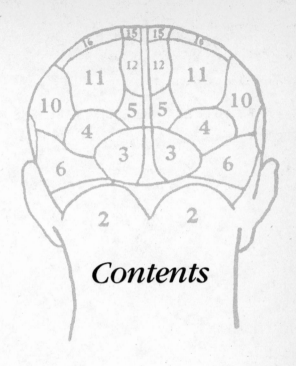

Contents

PART ONE: KEEPING THE BRAIN FIT

PART TWO: EXERCISING THE BRAIN

PART ONE

Keeping the Brain Fit

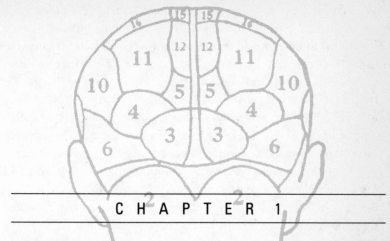

Making Your Brain Smarter

Let's look at two possible scenarios for events that could occur in the course of a typical day at the office.

DURING a busy period at work, you are juggling personnel, profits, and future business plans. You feel overwhelmed and panicked. Then a vice president from a branch office who happens to be in town calls to say he'd like to drop by in a few minutes, thus giving you little lead time. After you hang up the phone, you suddenly cannot remember his name. Your secretary is out, so you dial the number of a colleague who has some dealings with this branch office. When she comes on the line, you draw a blank about what you wanted to ask her, so you hang up. The vice president knocks on your door.

You realize the only thing you can do is to go ahead and fake it—maybe his name will come to you from something he says.

In the middle of a conversation on branch relations, you stumble over the words and then confuse the current topic on travel allowances with a discussion on office perks you had ten years ago. He brings out a statistical analysis of a new market that you have trouble following: He seems to want you to do difficult on-the-spot calculations and to project these data too far into the future. You cannot force your mind to concentrate, because his logic escapes you. He discusses the spatial layout of a new branch office, but you feel disoriented. You are getting a headache from all the discussion, all the words. You think that if you were younger you could handle these demands better, but then you realize you are much too young to have brain degeneration and wonder whether *your* brain could be degenerating much faster than normal.

ALTERNATIVELY...

Once again you find yourself at your desk, juggling personnel, profits, and future business plans. A mass of data threatens, yet you can make sense out of it. You know you need only apply your powers: pure reason; analytic thought; creative problem solving. You find life challenging and rewarding. You are confident, the decisions flow, your business is running smoothly. People like you as a manager and they come to you for advice. Your opinions are solicited from above and below. The company not only wants you around, but it is depending on you, counting on you to keep it profitable into the next century.

A vice president from a branch office happens to be in town and calls to tell you he'd like to drop by, giving you little lead time. You smile with pleasure at your memory of his sense of humor and warmth. When he arrives you welcome him to your office. You are working on enhancing branch relations, and you convey to him that he is the perfect person with whom to discuss your project. He brings out a statistical analysis of a new market and you make some quick mental calculations and point out a trend that he hadn't foreseen. He is also opening a new branch office and wants your opinion on the spatial layout because you have a reputation for being facile with spatial orientation. On his way out, he remarks what a pleasure it is to deal with a quick-minded person like you.

THE CAPACITY FOR IMPROVEMENT

To say that we can learn at any age, that we are never too old to learn something new, is by now a cliché.

We can, however, go beyond the cliché: An adult mind can not only acquire new knowledge, but improve its basic abilities to reason, solve problems creatively, perform mathematics, be fluent with language, and store and retrieve memories. Adult minds aren't limited to simple extensions of what we have already learned.

Nor are we restricted to the brain prowess we had at birth, or acquired during our early years, as neuroscientists used to think. Though it is true that we acquire our full complement of cortical neurons—the brain cells involved in the higher mental processes of thinking and perceiving—during the first half of gestation, our adult brains retain an extraordinary capacity for neural plasticity. The processes of neural plasticity may be different in the adult than in the developing child, whose nerve cells are still constructing their basic interconnections. However, adult neural plasticity is a characteristic of neural function throughout our life spans. Through use and practice, we can alter the connections (i.e., synapses) between nerve endings. Such changes result in new ways of sending and receiving neural signals among nerve cells, and, ultimately, an enhancement of our information-processing capacities.

For example, for each of the brain's overall functions (e.g., verbal or spatial processing), we can facilitate a more complex process called "learning-to-learn," in which we eliminate certain tendencies to make errors and acquire the ability to develop learning strategies. These "learning sets," as they are called, help us go beyond the solving of immediate problems to cope with problem solving of a more general nature. Instead of being fed a salmon, we are learning how to fish, thus enabling us to feed ourselves for a lifetime.

While we are acquiring these superordinate learning abilities, our neural circuits are acquiring an enhanced ability to juggle more neural information. Receptors, enzymes, and other functional proteins are being reorganized to handle the influx of new information. By exercising specific brain functions, we can propel them to new heights and empower ourselves. In short, we can improve our ability to improve.

A NEW WAY OF THINKING ABOUT THOUGHT

The neuroscience of the last twenty-five years or so has given us a new way to view the adult brain. Prior to this period, most of our insights about the brain came from turn-of-the-century discoveries by Nobel laureates Camillo Golgi and Santiago Ramón y Cajal, who focused their studies on the microanatomy of neurons (nerve cells). They showed that neurons have an arbor of dendrites—the message-receiving arms that really do look like naked trees in winter, and axons—the message-sending arms. It was from the brilliant studies conducted by these two men that we learned that our nervous systems operate by the signaling and receiving of messages from millions of individual neurons.

For decades, the research of biopsychologists and other neuroscientists was dominated by this emphasis on neurons as the source of intellectual power. Once we learned that no new neurons are added to a brain after gestation, we were led to the natural conclusion that whatever mental prowess a mature brain had acquired through its course of development was the approximate limit of an adult's ability. Adults could learn a few additional tricks, but because we couldn't acquire new nerve cells, we couldn't really enhance our basic intellectual functions. If our brain cells weren't stimulated to multiply further in fetal development, according to this premise, we had lost our chance at developing a larger intelligence.

This limited framework, with its focus on numbers of neurons, led to some conceptual anomalies, but these were simply excused with a verbal shrug of the shoulders. For example, if brain prowess was equated with the number of neurons a person had, then we should expect big-brained people to be smart and small-brained people to be less smart. Intellectual giants such as Walt Whitman and

Anatole France should have had extremely large brains, given their impact on society. But, as Stephen Jay Gould reports,[1] their brains weighed quite a bit less than the European average of 1300–1400 grams. Gould reports that in the late 1800s, eminent men were urged to donate their brains to science after death. Pioneering brain scientist Paul Broca (for whom the language circuits, Broca's area, were named) had been collecting craniometric results, with the thesis that the smarter fellows should have bigger brains. The results for such intellectual giants like Walt Whitman and Anatole France, being at the lower end of the range, were most disappointing and posed a problem for the general thesis. Broca was also hard pressed to account for a study of brain size in the 1850s by his German colleague Rudolf Wagner. Wagner had weighed the donated brains of dead professors at the University of Göttingen. The brain weights of these eminent men were nothing to crow about. By accounting for age and disease, Broca was able to recalculate the weights for some of these subaverage brains and thereby nudge the extrapolated weights up a bit. However, he couldn't find any brain calculation that "justified" their eminence. Reasoning backward, Broca eventually concluded that an important position at a major university was no guarantee of genius, and that even at a major university one was likely to find some unremarkable men.

Measuring brain weights to account for intellectual power (more

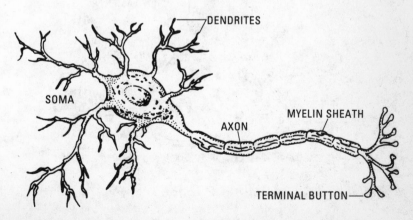

The microanatomy of a nerve cell, or neuron.

neurons, more processing power) declined when scientists realized that the major predictor of brain weight was body weight; larger bodies need larger brains to control them. That men have larger brains than women only means that they have larger bodies to control. It became obvious that the brain weight to body weight ratio —how much brain you have pound for pound—could be the only true predictor of intelligence, but even this ratio is useful only for comparison between large classes of animals (e.g., primates to other mammals). The ratio simply doesn't account for differences in human intelligence.

A new understanding of brain physiology was finally stimulated by research in the late 1960s and early 1970s, principally in the Swedish laboratories of Anders Bjorklund and Tomas Hokfeldt. They developed new methods of viewing the nervous system, allowing us to study the fine fiber systems of neurons we previously had not been able to see. One of the most exciting findings to emerge from these studies was that nerve *cells* may be fixed in an adult brain, but nerve *fibers* can be remodeled with an incredible amount of plasticity.

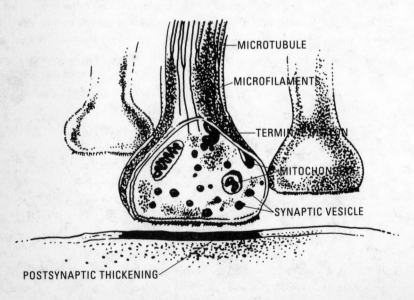

Diagram of the synapse, the functional unit of the nervous system.

The message unit was no longer the neuron, but the *synapse*—the connection between the sending and receiving fibers. It was now understood that it does not matter that the number of nerve cells are unchangeable, because the number of synapses and fine (previously unstudied) connecting fibers can be altered by experience.

This new neurophysiological model allowed us to see that brains continue to develop throughout our lives, not by the addition of neurons, but by the accumulation of experiences that change the chemistry and structure of our synapses. Brain exercise—a directed form of experience—is of value because it can change the functional abilities of the synapses between neurons. Through brain exercise, you have a way to change your pattern of interaction with the world.

THE NATURE-NURTURE DEBATE

Think back to the scenario at the beginning of this chapter in which the corporate executive was at the height of her powers. Powers like these are not a matter of chance; they are the result of stimulating the brain's functions and keeping it healthy and rewarded, well nourished and well rested. A brain with fluent language control develops in a person who regularly stimulates language circuits in her brain; a good memory for specifics develops in a person who has exercised her brain's memory functions; and the same holds true for elegant logic and creative abilities—these brain functions must be nurtured.

The ability to improve has been well demonstrated, but there remains a question about the degree to which one is limited by one's genetic endowment. Surely, a verbal wizard is born with a greater capacity for language development; the world's premier artists have special innate capacities to blend colors, construct forms, or arrange objects in space, and so forth. Are the rest of us doomed to mediocrity?

A legacy of the early brain researchers was the belief that a person's abilities—at least intellectual abilities—were largely hereditary. In short, your genetic material dictated the degree and nature of your talents based on the number of neurons in your brain. Many psychologists accepted this theory of innate intelligence and talent. Even psychologists who stayed away from strict genetic arguments, the nurturists, were prone to think that the "talents" you developed in early childhood (when the brain was still maturing) were the ones you possessed as an adult. The hidden assumption, of course, was that once you had attained full brain maturity, there wasn't much you could do to advance your talents.

This way of thinking about intellectual abilities became more rigidly fixed to a "nature," or genetic, argument when psychologists began to calculate the heritability of certain intellectual traits, especially IQ as measured on a standard intelligence test. One way to do this is to derive a mathematical index of heritability based on a comparison of correlations of IQ for individuals of differing genetic relatedness (e.g., identical twins are more closely related than fraternal twins). The correlations range in strength between 0 and 1 (1 being a perfect correlation) and can be positive or negative depending on whether IQ goes up or down with the degree of relatedness.

The early findings of higher, positive correlations for individuals who were more genetically related were greeted warmly by proponents of the nature argument, who pronounced IQ to be almost perfectly heritable. Using faulty reasoning, they went on to assert that the "trait" of intelligence was fixed. After all, they reasoned, if it was heritable, it must be fixed. Thus, what a person had in the way of intelligence was all a person would ever have.

But there are a number of problems with this argument, mostly related to the fact that a heritability estimate neither refers to the individual nor to differences between groups. If we take a less controversial trait like height for comparison, we can show that it, too, has a high degree of heritability (about 90 percent). That heritability estimate applies equally to the average height of adult U.S. males and adult males from virtually any third-world country, despite the fact that U.S. males are taller on the average. Thus, although we can say that height, as a trait, is heritable, we must grant that environmental variables such as better nutrition can act to determine the final expression of that trait. Moreover, the heritability estimate refers only to the variability within a population and not to a single individual. As noted psychologist Henry Gleitman has argued, heritability "does not mean that a man whose height is six feet can thank heredity for sixty-five of his inches and credit environment with the remaining seven."[2]

If that weren't enough to cast doubt on the notion of fixed, predetermined intellectual abilities, recent studies of IQ indicate a lower value for its heritability. The early estimates had shown that IQ was about 64–75 percent heritable. More recent estimates bring the range down to 25–49 percent,[3] leaving quite a lot of room for something other than genetics to influence IQ. Even if we concede the data in recent twin studies showing that identical twins reared apart are likely to have similar IQ ranges, we must also accept the data showing a strong impact of socioeconomic pressures on IQ.

There are a number of components to the "something other." Consider, for example, the role of the receptor proteins in intelligence. Depending on the particular neurotransmitter system, a brain with a larger number of receptor proteins could act on information flow faster than a brain with fewer. (In some neurotransmitter systems, exactly the opposite is true: Fewer receptor proteins may enhance information flow.) While the number of receptor proteins that your genes code for (and your neurons therefore produce) is in part determined by your inborn genetic complement (nature), the genes themselves reside in a fluid environment that can be altered by changes in diet and drug intake. Hence the instructions for protein production issued by your genes are subject to these external influences (nurture). But diet and drugs are not the only such external influences. We still have to consider the way in which the quantity of *information flow* also affects the brain cells' manufacture of proteins.

But how can this be? How can the amount of information flowing through your brain cells determine the amount of receptor proteins manufactured by them?

The answer lies in the means by which neurons send and receive information. Signals are sent via neurotransmitters—the chemical communicators in the brain. As far as the brain is concerned, information *is* chemistry. By means which will be discussed in part two, which explains the concept of brain exercise, the amount of "infor-

mation flow," or the "load," affects the production of neurotransmitters, which in turn affects the neurons' manufacture of receptor
proteins, ion channels, enzymes, and other proteins. These changes
determine how large a "load" can be processed. "Use it or lose it"
is one way of summarizing these principles. More positively, the
more you make use of your brain cells, the better they will perform.

Due to what we are now learning about the effects of not only
exercise (or "use"), but of nutrition, alcohol and drugs, and rest and
reward on brain power, we know that there is no single determinant
of intelligence, spatial ability, creativity, verbal fluency, or math wizardry. Genes affect but do not define the limits of one's abilities.
And the instructions that issue from the genes can themselves be
altered. Nature and nurture are so intermingled in the brain that it
is virtually useless to talk about their separate contributions. How
one aspect of "nurture" (exercise) can help one to enhance one's
genetic inheritance is the subject of the rest of this chapter. The other
major components of "nurture" will be discussed in the following
three chapters.

BUILDING BRAIN MUSCLES

If you perform Jane Fonda's workout for any length of time, you
gradually see improvement in calf and thigh muscles and in other
parts of the body. This improvement, which occurs as a result of a
process of adaptation, validates the workout.

When I first started training for a marathon, my legs looked like
normal legs. They weren't fat, but they weren't particularly fit, either.
One night after a long run I took a bath rather than my usual shower.
When I looked down at my legs, I was surprised that they had begun
to take on muscle definition. They looked as if they were fit to
perform, and I felt a keen sense of accomplishment.

Less than twenty years ago, scientists were surprised to learn
that brain cells act very much like muscle cells. The same proteins
muscle cells use for contraction—actin and myosin—are used by
brain cells to release their packets of chemicals for communication.
Another similarity between muscle and brain cells is their use of
calcium, sodium, and chemical energy (in the form of ATP, a phos-

phate-rich compound) to aid in the contraction coupling of actin and myosin. Moreover, muscle and brain cells both respond to neural signals to do their respective jobs.

In the context of a comparison between muscle and brain cells, it is particularly interesting to note that the intense training athletes undergo to improve muscle function increases the efficiency of oxygen and fuel use by those muscles; a similar increase in efficiency happens in the well-exercised brain. Research by Richard Haier at the University of California at Irvine shows that people who perform well on tests of abstract reasoning, "logic athletes," have brains that use chemical energy more efficiently than people with low scores.

If we define exercise as the repeated use of a muscle to handle a load, with the goal being to enable that muscle to bear an increased load, this gives us another point of comparison between muscle exercise and brain exercise. In the context of the brain, a "load" would be defined as the amount of information processed by a neural circuit. In the brain, exercise is the repeated use of a neural circuit to handle a gradually increased "load" of information.

Neurons, like muscle cells, adapt to such repetition. One kind of adaptation occurs when neurons produce greater amounts of an enzyme that helps them manufacture more neurotransmitters. In the simple sense, an unexercised neuron is much like a muscle cell before exercise. If you put a load (of information) on it, it (the neuron) depletes its contents of neurotransmitters, thereby tiring easily. As you continue to exercise it with repeated loads, however, it begins to adapt by producing greater amounts of the enzyme that will ensure it has more neurotransmitters. Once the neuron has adapted to exercise, the information load it is handling will not deplete its neurotransmitters so easily, and it will become capable of handling a larger load.

Neural adaptation can be called a "memory" of the demands we place on these brain circuits, because the neurons now "know" how to process additional information loads. And like muscle cells, neurons also have many other means of adapting to exercise. Proteins on the receiving end of a neural message can undergo a long-term positive chemical change, increasing their receptivity to subsequent volleys of information. The increased information flow produced by brain exercise can also enhance the sprouting of new nerve endings and dendrites, providing a greater number of connections to handle the additional neural information. And this is only a small sample of the possible neural responses to brain exercises.

Each intellectual task we perform develops its own memory as the neurons handling the tasks react to the mental stimulation. This cellular memory is a record of our level of using particular brain functions. As we ascend from one level of stimulation to the next, we have adapted the brain's neural circuits to the increased exercise. Although we don't see enhanced "muscle definition" in the brain, we do experience it.

HOW TO DEFINE BRAIN FUNCTIONS

If we are to discuss the exercising of specific brain functions, we have to be able to identify those functions. Unfortunately, one of the most difficult tasks biopsychologists face is how to classify the functions of the brain. We know approximately how many nerve cells the "average" brain has—there are over 100 trillion—and that each of these nerve cells may send out hundreds of nerve fibers. Individual nerve fibers may have hundreds of biochemical reactions, each one representing a brain "function" at some level. When all these factors are multiplied, the number of "functions" the brain has is truly astronomical.

However, when we talk about exercising "functions" of the brain, we don't have to deal with these minutiae. Our behavior is the collective result of the interactions among groupings of these small units. Neuroscientists have different ways of looking at these groupings. Some may focus on cell assemblies, while others observe neural networks or neurobehavioral systems. What makes this research particularly difficult is that any circuit controlling a brain function must communicate with circuits that interpret and express that function. For example, the language circuits that enable you to speak must communicate with the "simple motor circuits" that control movements of the mouth and tongue. Thus, most of the brain's functional systems are interconnected.

For the purpose of brain exercises, we don't have to understand the intricacies of this communication system. When we exercise a brain "function," we can count on millions of individual nerves and their fibers getting a workout—even if we don't have a clear picture of the physiology of these immensely complex events—and we can expect to enjoy the larger effects of that workout: an improvement in our problem-solving behaviors and an enhanced creativity.

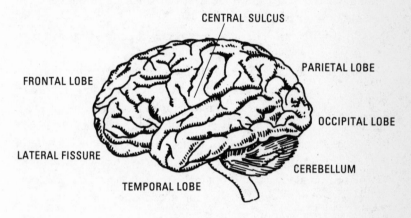

Side view of the left cerebral hemisphere (Gleitman's Psychology, p. 40)

We don't know exactly how many of these larger functions the brain has, but we do know a few good ways to group the functions for a fruitful discussion. One of the ways is to follow the lead of top psychologist Howard Gardner, and divide the intellect into superordinate functions.[4] Our brain's larger functions can be divided roughly into five main categories: language, spatial ability, logic, memory, and creativity. These larger functions can be defined as the things we do with our brains to deal effectively with our environments.

Language: We can all name some aspect of our job that requires verbal or written communication; improved language abilities would of course help with these particular needs. Going beyond the sheerly practical, noted author Salman Rushdie provides an eloquent description of the power and elasticity of language:

The real language problem: how to bend it, shape it, how to let it be our freedom, how to repossess its poisoned wells, how to master the river of words of time of blood.[5]

Language has several subfunctions that include the sounds of words, as well as the meaning, usage, and memory of words. Writers often say that to be good at what they do, they have to flex their writing muscles daily. As we improve our language abilities, we can become quicker and more facile with words. We can also convey our ideas more easily, because the means of conveyance will have become more efficient.

Brain circuits usually housed in the left external cortical portions of our brains (the brain matter inside the head area just forward of the top half of the left ear) enable us to understand and produce language; these are the primary circuits that will be further developed by increased language use. Broca's area, on the middle left side of the brain's frontal lobe, contains the circuits of language expression. Wernicke's area, toward the upper back of the left temporal lobe, processes and interprets language input, enabling us to comprehend written and oral communication.

Spatial Ability: This intellectual function involves so many of our interactions with the world, it is difficult to separate it from other functions. Our brains are performing spatial processing every time we get up from our desks and walk to the door, or look up and see the world around us. But in our daily lives we often have more specific spatial tasks to perform. When we need to assemble a toy for a child, take apart a small appliance, or choose the right location for the new living room couch, we are utilizing our spatial abilities to solve inherently spatial problems. Any task that requires us to interpret graphics, visualize the relation of a whole to its parts, or find locations entails the use of spatial abilities. Works by visual artists and sculptors represent the highest functioning of these abilities, but all of us can benefit from enhanced performance in the spatial world.

If you place your hand on the middle of the top of your head, it will lie over the (cortical) brain matter active in processing this function, but deeper areas in a structure called the hippocampus also store spatial memories. These areas of the brain that enable us to deal with spatial concepts must also be connected to visual processing and motor circuits to allow us to comprehend and move around in the world that surrounds us.

Logic: Logic involves thinking events through to their natural conclusions. It therefore entails a prediction of the future based on present or past experiences. When we develop our logic abilities, we become better able to discern the truth of conclusions others make. We can also avoid jumping to conclusions ourselves, and we are thus better able to take a reasoned approach to solving problems. The extremes of logic development are represented in philosophers, scientists, mathematicians, and programmers, but we can all benefit from a more analytical approach to problem solving.

No one brain area controls logic; it is a product of the workings of the entire brain. But we could look at this another way and say that each particular brain function requires a logic of its own. Our language functions, for example, require that we organize our verbal thoughts in a proper order. To write this book I need to be able to organize words in sentences, sentences in paragraphs, and paragraphs within chapters which are devoted to different topics. To be able to write also requires a certain motor logic. (I won't pound on the keyboard before I turn on the computer.) Within the hierarchy of logic operations these examples may be at low levels, but all higher logic operations depend on lower level processing for their completion. Thus, each brain function on which you are drawing for your particular logic must communicate with several other brain functions to get the job done.

Memory: Like logic, memory is a product of the workings of the entire brain, because memories must reside in each functional circuit of the brain. For example, language abilities depend on the memory of words and sentence structure housed in the same neural circuits that control language functions. Our logic and spatial abilities also depend on memories of past experiences and of objects in space, respectively. When we exercise these abilities, we strengthen our memories within each brain function. Different memory exercises targeted to various brain functions thus improve the brain circuits which control these functions. And if we target several different functions, memory exercises can improve the entire brain.

Creativity: Creativity is also a product of the workings of the entire brain, but there is still so little understanding of creativity that scientists have trouble defining it. We do know that creativity involves seeing the usual things in unusual ways, making unexpected combinations of conventional elements, and wresting unity out of disorder. Though some people believe that artists have a monopoly on creativity, we are all capable of it. Moreover, we can all exercise and enhance our innate capacity for creative thought. In doing so, we improve our abilities not only in solving problems but also in finding the right problems to solve. With creative exercise, we can stimulate the power of our brains to produce new ideas.

TAPPING YOUR BRAIN'S RESOURCES— HOW TO MEASURE

It is one thing to exercise your brain, but it is quite another to be able to discern the improvement. As you come to know the "feel" of your brain's individual functions, you will more easily be able to assess the status of your ability to use them and how various exercises affect them. Experiencing your improvement in a direct, palpable way makes you feel good, and that can be worth a high coin in esteem and assertiveness; but it is also nice to have an objective gauge of the results of your exercise program. After all, aerobic exercise makes you feel good, too, but exercise physiologists have ways of *measuring* your improvement by demonstrating that the program decreased your baseline heart rate and increased your endurance.

Fortunately, scientists in psychology have also developed techniques that enable us to see the net behavioral result of our brain improvements. By using these techniques to witness improvement, we avoid having to examine the neurochemistry directly; on the basis of what we can measure behaviorally, we are virtually guaranteed that the corresponding inner biochemical events have occurred.[6]

Our brains are linked to the outside world by our sensory equipment. Brains can see, hear, smell, taste, and touch what the body's senses give them in the way of processed nerve information.

Brains then respond to the outside world by directing the ways we walk, talk, and otherwise behave. If we change the ability of our brains to deal with incoming information, we alter the ways our brains instruct our bodies to behave. In essence, an improved brain function results in more effective management of our body's interaction with the outer world.

It is easy to measure the results of the brain's instructions to the body. What we want to know is whether a given brain function is taking place faster, with greater ultimate capacity, or with fewer errors in calculation.

One of the best measurements is *reaction time*—how fast we react to information. Examples of reaction time include: the speed of reply during a difficult conversation, quickness on the uptake in a logical debate, the speed of association of a face with a name. We can respond to information in as little as 100 milliseconds (one tenth of a second). However, this mental speed can vary widely, and it is this variation that makes it so useful as a measurement tool. As we improve neural circuits through directed exercise, mental speed is among the first of the "visible" measures that improve. If we let our brains slide through lack of exercise, mental speed deteriorates.

Another concrete measurement of brain function is *time to completion*—essentially the time it takes to solve a problem. This is related to mental speed, but it is more easily measured; a stopwatch will do. The time it takes to calculate a sales commission, to analyze what your opponent's logical reply should be, or to locate the best placement of a desk in your office are all examples of this kind of measurement. The faster you complete these tasks, the more indication you have of improvement in the relevant neural circuits.

A third measurement is the *number of errors* made in solving a problem. Errors are of many kinds. You may make a false start when you are starting to work on a problem, or get temporarily lost in a cul-de-sac during the solving of the problem. Wasted motion can also be considered an error when fluidity and direction of movement are the goals. As a brain function improves, the outcome is often measured in decreases in wasted movement and false starts.

These improvements, by the way, can also reflect our *learningto-learn*. As we exercise various functions of the brain, our ability to efficiently solve more of our daily tasks increases. Our brains have improved when we are better able to classify several tasks under similar problem headings. We are able to get more things done when we train our brains to recognize the unity in problems. Thus, as our spatial abilities improve, we begin to see that understanding a new office arrangement is similar, in brain functioning, to designing an effective graphics presentation. We have trained our spatial functions to recognize a set of spatial problems that we can easily solve, no matter how different they may seem on the surface.

The exercises in this book are constructed so that you can use these measurement tools to heighten your awareness of brain improvement. You will begin to see changes whether you do brief daily exercises (perhaps during your commute) or you train as though for a brain olympics contest. As your brain functions increase in power, you will be getting faster and making fewer mistakes during exercise, and you will begin to notice improvement in all the daily tasks you perform.

THE GHOST IN THE MACHINE

Up to now, we have described the workings of the brain as a process in which raw information enters a thinking machine, gets rearranged as it travels through the neural circuits, and then comes out again in better form once the machine has "massaged" it. As far as it goes, it's not a bad description. But it doesn't even attempt to touch on the relation between brain and mind.

Francis Crick, one of the Nobel laureates who discovered the structure of DNA, once had a discussion about brains with a friend of his. He asked her how she thought she saw the world. She replied that somewhere in her head she thought she had the equivalent of a little television set. "So who," Crick asked, "is looking at it?"

Who, indeed! Who is it looking at your perceptions of the world? What is it that sets your fingers into motion so you can play the piano or lift a pen? If you say that nerves set your fingers into motion, I would have to ask, "Who is instructing those nerves?"

At stake here is how the physical properties of our brains—nerves, fibers, chemicals—control the entity we call the mind. To

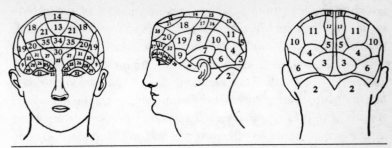

MEASURING TALENTS BY FEELING BUMPS ON THE SKULL

Fig. 1 The "Powers and Organs of the Mind," According to Spurzheim, Phrenology, or the Doctrine of Mental Phenomena, *1834.*

AFFECTIVE FACULTIES

PROPENSITIES	SENTIMENTS
? Desire to live	10 Cautiousness
* Alimentiveness	11 Approbativeness
1 Destructiveness	12 Self-Esteem
2 Amativeness	13 Benevolence
3 Philoprogenitiveness	14 Reverence
4 Adhesiveness	15 Firmness
5 Inhibitiveness	16 Conscientiousness
6 Combativeness	17 Hope
7 Secretiveness	18 Marvelousness
8 Acquisitiveness	19 Ideality
9 Constructiveness	20 Mirthfulness
	21 Imitation

INTELLECTUAL FACULTIES

PERCEPTIVE	REFLECTIVE
22 Individuality	34 Comparison
23 Configuration	35 Causality
24 Size	
25 Weight and Resistance	
26 Coloring	
27 Locality	
28 Order	
29 Calculation	
30 Eventuality	
31 Time	
32 Tune	
33 Language	

Examining the surface of the skull used to be an accepted way of measuring the brain's "talents." In the late 1800s brain scientists toyed with phrenology, the science of determining a person's character and mental faculties by an analysis of bumps on the skull. The idea was that your skullcase had grown over parts of the brain specially developed for particular functions. If the bone was elevated over a brain area—if you had a bump—then you were supposed to have a special "talent" because of the extra development of underlying brain matter. Though the theory has long since fallen into general disuse, only a few years ago you could walk into a Bourbon Street shop in New Orleans and have what looked like a complicated beauty parlor hair dryer placed over your head to "feel" the bumps. When your skull was "read," your character was interpreted according to the old phrenology method.

return to the television metaphor, if we do have a little television set in our heads, the question is how our brain cells can produce and act in the shows and *watch* them at the same time.

We often glimpse the workings of our minds: We can think about what we are thinking, feeling, or perceiving. We know when our brains are tired and when they seem to be operating really well. We also have dreams and memories that we can discuss with others by converting the images into a useful and readily understood language. But it's difficult to reconcile the almost magical qualities of thoughts, dreams, emotions and memories with the sheerly electrochemical activities of cells and fibers in our brain matter. The evidence for mind as a physical phenomenon is overwhelming, however.

One of the giants of neurosurgery, Wilder Penfield, was the first person to explore the minds of conscious human beings, beginning in the late 1920s. In doing so, he demonstrated persuasively that minds reside in the physical entities of our brains. Penfield's research was based on his work with severely epileptic patients, who have uncontrollable convulsions because of electrochemical storms raging in their brains. As a neurosurgeon, one of Penfield's efforts on behalf of these patients was to find the epileptic focus—the site where the storm builds up. To do this, he had to probe his patients' brains with an electric pen. During this probing, the patients were awake and talking.

What made this operation possible is that the brain does not feel sensation as the rest of the body does. Once Penfield cut through the anesthetized scalp and bone, he could probe the brain while asking his patients what they were thinking and feeling.

When he touched the probe to portions of the temporal lobe, a few patients immediately saw vivid images or heard musical tones stored in their memories. One patient heard a church concert as she had heard it years ago. Her flashback was so vivid that she felt as if it were real. Another patient reported a familiar memory of being in an office where "I could see the desks. I was there and someone was calling to me—a man leaning on his desk with a pencil in his hand."[7] Penfield thus showed us that what we put into our brains resides there until called out from "storage."

It is remarkable to realize that what we put into storage—whether tiny concrete facts or sensual, resonant memories—becomes a part of the biochemical structure of our brains. Brains are changed by what we put into them. Brain exercise is simply a way of inputting material that will change them for the better.

LEVELS OF BRAIN PROWESS

As you begin to understand your brain's nature—how it goes about controlling various aspects of your life—you will begin to see ways in which you can exploit that nature to suit your needs. You will learn to pick and choose the brain functions you want to enhance now, and save the improvement of other brain functions for the times you need them most.

It is important to realize that you do not need a high level of brain power to improve specific brain functions. In fact, it is better not to think in terms of overall brain power while you are learning how to perform brain exercises. You are not working on your IQ so much as enhancing specific abilities of your brain to perform in certain desirable ways. If your IQ improves, so much the better, but the real goal is to change your life by improving the functions of your brain.

In this regard, the analogy to athletic exercise still provides the best illustration. Whatever your level of athletic ability, you can exercise specific muscle groups and systems to improve any physical function. If you want to improve your ability to run, you would not distribute your exercises to build all the muscles of the body. You would focus primarily on strength and endurance of running muscles and fitness of the cardiovascular system. You may improve overall athleticism as a happy by-product of your focus—and become better in tennis or another sport—but you will satisfy your particular needs faster and with less waste by performing the exercises specific to those needs.

You do not have to attain the brain equivalents of Steffi Graf's or Michael Jordan's level of physical fitness to be quicker in conversation, better at solving problems, have richer memories and livelier associations, and have better ideas and be better able to communicate them to others. Brain exercise can help you have a more fruitful intellect whether you are at the top or bottom of your profession. You only have to want to improve.

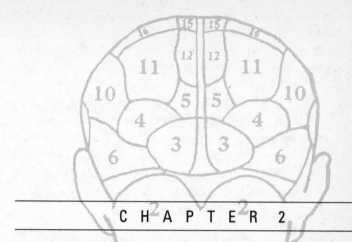

CHAPTER 2

Eating the Right Brain Foods: Nutrients for Brain Exercise

As you engage in brain exercises, you will be stimulating your brain's neural plasticity—the ability of nerve cells and connecting fibers to undergo biochemical and structural changes. But these changes are chemically expensive; they require brain cells to use large amounts of chemical energy and nutrients.

Brain cells live in a rich medium of biochemicals. Their ability to make the changes deriving from brain exercise depends in part on the supply of nutrients they extract from this medium. If certain nutrients are plentiful, neurons have little difficulty producing new neurotransmitter materials or building up an additional supply of enzymes or receptors—all the changes that enhance your brain power. If these nutrients are absent or in low supply, neurons have a harder time producing what you need to adapt to the rigors of brain exercise.

Whether or not you deliberately exercise it, the brain also requires an adequate nutritional supply for its normal, everyday functions. Many of the nutrients necessary for these functions—for the synthesis of certain neurotransmitters—aren't manufactured in the body; they must be provided in the diet. Inadequate nutrition can thus lead to impairments of thought processes and other basic brain functions. So although it is a cliché to say "you are what you eat," it is certainly true that your brain cells cannot conduct their optimum biochemical business without a complete set of nutrients on which to draw.

RECOMMENDED DIETARY ALLOWANCES

What constitutes good nutrition? Basic guidelines can be found in the Recommended Dietary Allowances (RDAs) established by the Food and Nutrition Board of the National Research Council. The Board defines RDAs as "the levels of intake of essential nutrients that, on the basis of scientific knowledge, are judged by [the Board] to be adequate to meet the known nutrient needs of practically all healthy persons."[1] This definition does not include individuals with special nutrient needs and has, according to the Council, been essentially unchanged since 1974.

RDAs are based on a number of different kinds of scientific observations. Some of these are actual experiments performed on subjects who have volunteered to ingest deficient diets or to have their nutrient status monitored in relation to intake. Other kinds of observations include epidemiological (the study of disease prevalence) monitoring of nutrient status in large groups of people. For some nutrients, biochemical events are studied in various tissues to determine rates of nutrient saturation or molecular function. In some cases in which data from people are not available, a careful extrapolation from animal experiments is employed. The RDAs can change from year to year as new research makes it clear that lower or higher values are needed for adequate maintenance or functioning of tissues. (Actually, many of the values for 1989 were lowered from 1988.)

In essence, the RDAs represent the Food and Nutrition Board's most informed guess about nutrient values that will maintain health and prevent depletion. But because the data come from so many different kinds of observations, and because nutrients have varying functions in different tissues, the RDA may refer only to the amount of a nutrient necessary to prevent a tissue function from weakening. This nutrient level could be very different from the one required to maintain adequate storage in the body.

The upshot is that different tissues (i.e., the brain) may require levels of nutrients for optimum functioning that differ from the published RDAs. It is not that the RDAs are wrong, but that every possible function for every nutrient cannot be examined, and the Board has to stop somewhere. For example, the published RDA for vitamin C in both men and non-pregnant women (all non-smokers) is 60 milligrams per day (mg/day). This value takes into account the body pool "buffer" that would prevent scurvy for thirty days if a person were to quit ingesting the vitamin. But prevention of scurvy is not the only function of the vitamin. Vitamin C interacts with dopamine, one of the brain's neurotransmitters, to control a person's body movements. Vitamin C is also important for the manufacture of hormones by the pituitary and adrenal glands.

No one really knows the optimal level of vitamin C for the brain's behavioral functions. If we examine the range of vitamin C production in animals who can manufacture it (and therefore don't need to supplement their diets), we find that animals make 44 to 306 times the amounts we need just to buffer against scurvy (the RDA). This suggests that the RDA is certainly not the value needed to optimize all functions—including the brain's—but we will simply have to live with the RDAs until research suggests we should adopt a different value.

As I suggested earlier, however, the Food and Nutrition Board does take into account various factors—e.g., pregnancy and smoking—that necessitate a greater intake of a nutrient. (Smoking leads to less than optimal brain power, but if you do smoke you should at least be aware of your greater nutritional needs.) Where appropriate, I will indicate these higher values. For optimum brain functioning, you should make sure you take in the RDAs, but I will also show the specific circumstances in which the brain might require an immediate nutrient fix. With this information, you can change the pattern of your acquisition of the RDAs to optimize your brain power.

NUTRITION FOR THE BRAIN

All cells—brain, heart, liver, skin, muscle—need three basic *macronutrients* for growth and normal activity. *Proteins* provide components—amino acids—that enable your cells to assemble their own proteins. *Carbohydrates* (sugars and starches) are necessary for the chemical energy they provide. *Fats* and oils are used to form hormones and other important chemicals for cell communication, and they contribute to energy storage.

Proteins

Proteins are necessary constituents of a cell's biochemical activity. In brain cells, proteins have roles as enzymes, pumps, channels, gates, receptors, and structural elements. Proteins acting in these roles help brain cells manufacture neurochemicals, conduct neural signals, and react to neural transmissions. Additionally, when neurons are stimulated by brain exercise to produce new nerve terminals and receiving fibers (dendrites), they must manufacture proteins to support the extra neural signaling and transmission demanded by this growth.

We do not acquire these specialized proteins in the diet; our brain cells manufacture all the proteins they need to conduct their neural business. Any proteins we do eat are digested first and never reach the brain in their original form anyway.

However, to manufacture the brain's proteins, brain cells must chain together *amino acids*,[2] the "building blocks" of proteins, according to a code specified in the cells' genetic machinery.

Fourteen of the twenty-two amino acids used in the building of brain proteins can be manufactured by chemical processes in cells. We should acquire these in the diet to replace what is lost in chemical turnover and other bodily losses (excretions and sloughed skin and hair), but these amino acids are not needed from the diet for the immediate dynamics of chemical reactions. The eight remaining amino acids (nine, in children) are called "essential," because they must be acquired in the diet for maintenance of health and tissue function and normal growth. Two of these essential amino acids—tryptophan and phenylalanine—are required by the brain to manufacture neurotransmitters. If they are lacking in the diet, brain function can deteriorate rapidly.

EIGHT ESSENTIAL AMINO ACIDS (L-FORM)

Amount in Foods

relatively abundant	*relatively scarce*
phenylalanine	lysine
threonine	isoleucine
leucine	methionine
valine	tryptophan

The biologic value of the proteins we eat is determined by the kinds and amounts of amino acids contained in the proteins. High protein foods that are of the highest biologic value include eggs, milk, fish, meat, and poultry. These foods contain adequate amounts of all of the essential amino acids, plus substantial amounts of the nonessential amino acids.

A protein with one of the lowest biologic values is gelatin. Gelatin lacks valine and tryptophan, and it is deficient in the nonessential amino acids, tyrosine and cystine. Proteins obtained from plants—wheat, rice, corn, beans, nuts—generally have lower biologic values than animal proteins. The value of plant proteins can be boosted considerably, though, by eating them in a mixed variety, a fact long known to cultures offering a mixture of corn or rice and beans at meals. Benjamin Burton, the author of *Human Nutrition*,[3] reports that a mixture of corn, sorghum, cottonseed meal, and torula yeast has been used in Central America as a treatment for protein deficiency.

The biologic value of even high-value proteins can be affected by the method of cooking, which can alter their digestibility. In general, overcooking (well-done) can destroy the more heat-sensitive amino acids, and cooking in dry heat (baking) or oil (frying) can cross-link some of the chemical bonds in proteins, rendering them indigestible. In practice, however, as long as you don't overcook all protein sources, and you maintain an adequate variety of proteins, as well as cooking methods, you will be able to supply your brain with the requisite amino acids.

The RDAs for protein have been unchanged for decades. The Food and Nutrition Board of the National Research Council recommends that women consume 44–50 grams and men 45–63 grams daily. Pregnant or lactating women need 60–65 grams. A comprehensive cookbook such as *The Joy of Cooking* will give you the protein values in average servings of most of the foods we eat. These values are taken from public information provided by the U.S. Department of Agriculture. A few examples of high-quality protein foods are given in the table below.

SOME SOURCES OF HIGH-QUALITY PROTEIN

Source	*Amount* (grams)
egg (1 whole)	6.3
milk (1 cup whole)	8.0
milk (1 cup skim)	9.3
shrimp, boiled (5 large)	15.5
cottage cheese (½ cup)	17.0
pork chop (3½ oz)	21.4
lake trout (3 oz)	21.5
roast beef (3 oz)	23.3
chicken breast (3½ oz)	32.3
tuna, canned (½ cup)	36.4

You should not think that if the RDA amounts are good for you, then greater amounts would be even better. For one thing, as Marion Nestle reports in *Nutrition in Clinical Practice*,[4] the estimated average protein intake of U.S. adults is 101 grams per day, so we are likely to be getting more than we need anyway. Moreover, high protein diets for prolonged periods may even be harmful, and have been associated with excess mineral loss.

Carbohydrates

The carbohydrates with the simplest chemical structures are the simple sugars. The three simple sugars most important to human nutrition are glucose, fructose, and galactose. The chemical energy that fuels the brain's communication and protein manufacturing processes comes almost exclusively from glucose. In fact, the brain usually extracts glucose from the bloodstream faster than any other organ. Moreover, when the brain is exercised, it utilizes glucose (for energy) at a faster rate than normal. If that glucose is not available in the bloodstream, your brain cannot operate at peak efficiency.

More complex sugars are composed of two simple sugars. The best known example is sucrose (table sugar), which is made of an equal proportion of glucose and fructose. Lactose, or milk sugar, is composed of glucose and galactose. Maltose, a component of beer, contains two units of glucose.

Complex carbohydrates are formed as long chains of simple sugars. Starches are the digestible complex carbohydrates. Digestion breaks these down into simple sugars, which are then absorbed for use as metabolic fuels. Though it is not conclusive (and though it may seem contrary to common sense), recent evidence indicates that ingestion of starches—despite their more complex form—may produce a faster rise in blood sugar than sugars.

The major natural sources of carbohydrates are fruits, vegetables, and cereals. Potatoes and foods based on cereals (bread and pasta) supply a great proportion of the carbohydrates we ingest. Compounded foods such as cakes and pies give us heavy doses of starches and sugars. It is these sweetened foods that usually figure in our overconsumption, which when exceeding our energy needs shifts our metabolism to store the excess as fat.

If we were not concerned with the sources of our body's energy, we would not strictly need to ingest any carbohydrate. This is because glycerol, a component of fats, and some amino acids can be converted to glucose. In the absence of carbohydrate intake, fats are also metabolized to produce ketones, which the brain can use for immediate energy. Prolonged ketone formation, however, produces a dangerous condition known as ketosis, in which toxic levels of ketones build up. Moreover, under these conditions, the amino acids used to produce energy may be taken from the breakdown of body protein. (Those of you on a diet that restricts carbohydrate intake should note that some dietary carbohydrates are necessary to spare the breakdown of body protein.) As Marion Nestle reports, ingestion of 150–250 grams of carbohydrates per day prevents these deleterious effects. The following table taken from data supplied by the U.S. Department of Agriculture shows the amounts of carbohydrates contained in some common foods.

CARBOHYDRATE CONTENT OF SOME COMMON FOODS

Food	Amount (grams)
zucchini squash (1 cup)	4.5
milk, whole (1 cup)	12.0
milk, skim (1 cup)	12.5
corn (1 ear)	16.2
cookies (4 choc. chip, homestyle; 2.3 in. dia.)	24.0
bread, wheat (2 slices—soft crumb)	27.6
bread, white (2 slices—soft crumb)	28.2
banana (1 large)	30.2
apple (1 large)	30.7
potato (1 whole baked)	32.8
cola beverage (12 oz.)	36.9
pasta (1 cup cooked macaroni)	39.1
cake (white, iced; 1 piece)	59.7

Two Sweeteners

Fructose is sweeter than table sugar and is used to sweeten many foods and drinks because of its high taste appeal. Fruits and honey are the major natural sources of fructose, but they usually contain high proportions of other sugars such as glucose.

Fructose can be used for energy in most tissues; in fact, it is an initial step in the energy-releasing breakdown of glucose. But, not only does the brain lack the enzymes to extract the energy from fructose, fructose cannot even get into the brain. Because the brain cannot get energy from fructose, you should be careful of foods sweetened with it, especially in the late morning or afternoon when your blood sugar is running low. If you have an important meeting at these times, consuming a food or drink sweetened with fructose could leave you flat and unimpressive.

If you need a charge of energy but don't want the high influx of calories contained in a candy bar, try eating a few crackers, some melba toast, or a small apple. These foods contain complex carbohydrates that provide a quick and sustained release of energy. Remember, you can enjoy honey on your bran muffin or a fructose-sweetened drink later; they won't harm your brain, but neither will they help it much. If you are concerned about mental performance, eat foods rich in energy sources the brain can use.

Aspartame, the chemical compound of which NutraSweet is made, is not a carbohydrate, but it is considered here because aspartame replaces conventional sugars in many diet foods and drinks. Aspartame is actually composed of two of the building blocks (amino acids) of protein—phenylalanine and aspartate.

Phenylalanine may be an essential amino acid, but it is also the amino acid that gives people who have phenylketonuria (PKU) so much trouble. These people lack the enzyme that metabolizes phenylalanine, so their levels of this amino acid build up. When this happens, they have trouble thinking and performing other mental tasks.

But the deleterious mental effects of phenylalanine may not be limited to people who have PKU. It is possible for anyone to consume aspartame so quickly that the converting enzyme is overwhelmed and can't handle the rapid influx of phenylalanine. And a brain loaded with extra phenylalanine that it can't convert quickly enough won't operate at its peak—or anywhere close to it. You could end up with symptoms of PKU without having the disease.

Noted researcher Paul Spiers studied the mental effects of aspartame in people who had consumed the FDA's maximum allowable limit.[5] When subjected to a demanding and self-paced computer test of learning ability, people who had consumed high amounts of aspartame failed to improve and their performance often worsened. Although the research is not conclusive, the evidence does suggest that a rapid build up of phenylalanine (released when aspartame is digested) can have injurious effects on mental ability.

But the story is not over. To get into the brain, phenylalanine must compete with other amino acids. Therefore, one diet soda sweetened with aspartame, especially if you drink it during a high protein meal, most likely wouldn't provide enough phenylalanine to do your brain harm. But if you haven't had much to eat all day, and you drink several diet drinks, you won't have the physiological competition to keep phenylalanine out of your brain, and you risk a downturn in brain performance.

You could do yourself even greater harm if you eat carbohydrates (cakes or sweet snacks) along with diet drinks. Foods that contain carbohydrates set off a physiological cascade that helps boost phenylalanine's ability to get into the brain. By reducing its physiologic competition, these foods help the brain get an extra dose of phenylalanine—more than it would have gotten if you hadn't eaten carbohydrates.

Recommendations about aspartame are easily put into practice. Say you have a requirement for peak mental efficiency, such as a high-powered meeting or lecture, and you feel the need for a snack or a soft drink beforehand. A carbohydrate snack for quick energy —crackers or a candy bar—is fine as long as you don't wash it down with a diet drink containing aspartame. If you do intend to have a diet drink, however, your snack should include a form of protein— peanuts, cheese, yogurt—to offset the effects of the aspartame, rather than carbohydrates, which will only heighten the aspartame effects.

Remember, too, that it's not only diet drinks that contain aspartame. Some high-carbohydrate diet snacks are sweetened with it, and they can also cause a mind-dulling response—precisely the opposite of what you want when you need to perform well.

Fats

Fats, or lipids, are composed of chemical units called fatty acids. When an advertiser talks about "polyunsaturated" fats, it is generally meant to connote a healthier product—the fats are probably derived from vegetable sources—but technically it means that the fatty acids have a chemical bonding arrangement that excludes hydrogen atoms.

MEMORY FOOD

Paul Gold is one of the country's top scientists working on the nutritional physiology of memory. Gold has been researching the influence of adrenaline on memory and has found that slight to moderate increases in the secretion of adrenaline improve memory. Adrenaline is normally secreted into the bloodstream when you are aroused. Situations that are important to you, and are thus arousing, are therefore more easily remembered because of the enhanced levels of adrenaline.

One of the actions of adrenaline is to release stored-up blood sugar (glucose) for the energy you might need when you are aroused. The rise in physiological glucose made Gold wonder whether added dietary glucose might have an effect on memory. He tested elderly subjects who had a declining memory by giving them lemonade sweetened with either glucose or saccharin. The subjects who had consumed the glucose had improved memory performance. Gold suggested that the poor regulation of blood sugar among some elderly individuals may be an easily remedied cause of a declining memory.

Gold's work suggests that you should not attend an important meeting—especially if you are giving a presentation—in a state of low blood sugar. It is therefore best not to drink a sweet diet drink in place of breakfast, because you will be depriving your brain cells of energy-releasing glucose.[6]

By contrast, animal fats have a different chemical structure that allows "saturation" of hydrogens.

The lipids that we ingest are not soluble in water. Therefore, to be transported through the bloodstream, they must chemically combine with proteins to form lipoproteins. Several hours after a fatty meal, blood plasma has a milky appearance due to high concentrations of one class of lipoproteins.

We are frequently educated by health advocates about the relationship between our overconsumption of fat and its deleterious effects on the cardiovascular system. This is important to recognize because estimates indicate that we ingest four to five times the amount of fatty acids required to maintain health. This emphasis, though highly valuable in preventing disease, should not obscure the fact that fat is an integral part of our physiology and essential to our well-being.

The Food and Nutrition Board defines our need for fat in its requirement that we take in five grams of the essential fatty acid, linoleic acid, daily. To keep things in perspective, you should note that a cup of whole (cow) milk contains 8.5 grams total fat, but only 0.2 grams linoleic acid. The following table, constructed from data supplied by the U.S. Department of Agriculture, gives the total fat and linoleic acid content of some common foods. Note that the fat supplied from plant sources (*), compared with animal fats, usually gives much greater proportions of linoleic acid.

FAT CONTENT OF SOME COMMON HIGH-FAT FOODS

Source	Total Fat (grams)	Linoleic Acid (grams)
butter (1 pat)	4.1	0.1
* margarine (1 pat)	4.1	1.1
egg (1 large)	5.8	0.4
* peanut butter (1 Tbs.)	8.1	2.3
whole milk (1 cup)	8.5	0.2
cheddar cheese (1 oz.)	9.1	0.3
* safflower oil (1 Tbs.)	13.6	9.8
* pecans (1 oz.)	20.2	4.0
rich ice cream (1 cup)	23.8	0.7
ham (3 oz.)	26.0	2.3

* Fat supplied from plant sources.

In the brain (as well as in all body cells), linoleic acid is a major component of cell membranes. When new nerve terminals and receiver branches (dendrites) are formed as a result of brain exercise, more linoleic acid must be used to form the extra membrane surface.

Moreover, the brain's filter that keeps unwanted proteins and other substances from reaching the brain is made of similar fat-containing membranes. Fats are also used to form a broad class of hormones —steroids—that have widespread effects throughout the brain and body.

For the brain's ability to manufacture a major neurotransmitter, acetylcholine, which is important in the higher brain functions like memory and learning, a component of a fat called lecithin is needed. This component is choline.

The transmitter, acetylcholine, is so fundamental to your brain that if you lose the neurons that supply it, you'll develop Alzheimer's disease, a disorder accompanied by a profound loss of memory and cognitive ability. Although Alzheimer's disease itself still resists treatment, drugs that act chemically to stimulate the activity of acetylcholine in elderly patients who do not have Alzheimer's disease will improve their memory performance.

Supplemental choline can be used to change the amount of choline in the brain—the raw material used to manufacture acetylcholine. Choline has been used as a treatment for patients who have a brain disorder known as tardive dyskinesia, which causes uncontrolled chewing movements and is associated with low levels of acetylcholine. However, the choline produced a rather offensive side effect. Intestinal bacteria chemically altered the choline, changing it into a biochemical found in rotting fish. The patients had fewer symptoms of the brain disorder, but they smelled strongly of fish! Fortunately, changing the treatment to the compound form of choline—lecithin—rapidly eliminated the smell while alleviating symptoms of the disease.

Almost all the choline we consume in our diets is derived from lecithin.[7] The richest sources of dietary lecithin and choline are liver, eggs, soybeans, wheatgerm, and peanuts, although other animal and vegetable proteins contain significant amounts. Torula yeast, which is often added to foods as an emulsifier, and is available in health food stores, is another source of lecithin.

Because the brain can make its own choline, it is not strictly required in the diet. However, scientists have shown that the choline and lecithin we ingest have a much easier time being absorbed by an activated brain, as compared to a brain that is not being stimulated by exercise. This exciting research compels us to think of the co-ordination of diet and brain exercise. If we are not exercising the brain systems that use choline, the choline we ingest in our diets will not be readily absorbed by our brains and therefore will not do us much good. On the flip side of this argument, the more we exercise a brain that is well stocked with choline, the better we can make use of it for the regulation of our intellectual activities.

Dr. Judith Wurtman, M.I.T. scientist and one of the world's top experts on dietary effects on human behavior, recommends a treatment for those fuzzy afternoons when you are feeling absentminded or slow-witted and you need to perform: Try popping a few peanuts.[8] The added dietary lecithin is enough to give an effective boost to your brain's choline content. Remember, however, that the extra choline won't do you much good unless your brain is also being activated by brain exercise. So the most effective thing to do would be eating the peanuts while doing the brain exercises shown later in this book.

For those of you who want to avoid eating extra calories or fats while you are feeding your brain, dietary supplements of choline or lecithin are available (usually in your local health food outlet). If you do take these supplements, be sure to use an encapsulated form of choline or pure lecithin to avoid the fishy odor that can arise by eating pure choline. No requirement for choline is known, but doctors have prescribed 40–80 grams (1.4–2.8 oz.) per day (choline or lecithin) as a treatment for brain disorders involving acetylcholine. Remember that it is best to check with a physician first before supplementing your normal diet.

And be cautious about lecithin: Commercial manufacturers are allowed to call several related compounds "lecithin," but the only one that feeds your brain is *phosphatidylcholine* (phospha—as in phosphates; tidyl—as in a tidal wave; and choline). Impure lecithin contains some of the pure substance mixed in with other substances that don't enhance neural transmission the way pure lecithin does. So check the labels or ask at your local pharmacy or health food store.

Minerals and Trace Elements

The brain also requires certain minerals and trace elements for healthy functioning. Among the most important are sodium (table salt) and potassium, which the brain uses in every nerve cell to conduct its chemo-electric messages.

Most of us in the U.S. need not be concerned about adding sodium to our diets, however, but rather with monitoring our intake of it, since we are not at risk from deficits so much as from over-consumption; sodium is implicated in hypertension. We require about 200 milligrams daily (available in about ½ gram of table salt), but we consume 10–35 times that amount.[9] National Health and Nutrition Examination Surveys indicate that we ingest most of our sodium from white bread, rolls, crackers, hot dogs, ham, lunch meats, cheeses, and soups. Most of our potassium comes from coffee or tea, milk, potatoes, orange juice, beef, and bananas.

Sodium deficits can become a problem, however, if you spend a lot of time outdoors in hot climates (or otherwise sweat a lot). In these cases, your brain will tell you when you need to take a little extra salt by making you feel especially sluggish and slow-witted. Otherwise, you should add flavor to your food by experimenting with different spices rather than adding salt.

Another important dietary mineral is calcium, which is used in neurons the same way as in muscles—to enable the signaling proteins, actin and myosin, to interact. It is therefore quite important for neuronal signaling. The RDA for calcium in both men and women is 1200 milligrams. Foods with high levels of calcium include salmon, milk, yogurt, cheese, tofu (soybean curd), molasses, almonds, and broccoli.

Magnesium is also important for neural transmission and reception. Women need about 300 milligrams and men 350 milligrams daily. Pregnant and lactating women need as much as men. Foods that supply magnesium include tofu, lima beans, nuts, shredded wheat, bananas, molasses, potatoes, and spinach.

Of all the trace elements required for health, none has been more intensively researched with respect to its role in brain function than zinc (see companion box). Dietary deficiencies of zinc can lead to severe decrements in brain function. Zinc is important in neural transmission, and many neurobiologists now think that zinc may play a major role in the growth of new nerve endings.

ZINC MAY BE THE LINK

Zinc is absorbed from the blood supply into the outer cortical areas of the brain where the highest levels of mental performance—memory, language, reason, insight—are controlled. If neurons in these cortical brain areas do not have access to zinc, their functions begin to deteriorate, and they cannot be activated or stimulated as easily with brain exercise.

Several medical reports indicate the importance of dietary zinc for brain function. Harold Sandstead, one of the world's top experts on dietary zinc deprivation, reports that people who live in zinc-poor regions of the world have deterioration of mental functions that can be alleviated with treatments of zinc.[10] Another report indicates that a treatment for progressive systemic sclerosis caused patients to excrete the zinc they already had in their systems; these patients then developed memory loss and disorientation until they were treated for the zinc deficit. The mental signs of zinc loss disappeared within eight to twenty-four hours.

The RDA for zinc is 15 milligrams in men and 12 milligrams in women. Pregnant women need 15 milligrams and lactating women need 19–25 milligrams. Because zinc is secreted in sweat, athletes and people who work in hot climatic conditions should ingest up to 20 milligrams.

The highest levels of zinc are found in oysters and other shellfish. The levels of zinc in oysters are some 30–50 times (320 milligrams per 4 ounce serving) higher than their nearest competitors: The red meats (7 milligrams per 4 ounce serving). You can also obtain zinc from nuts, cheeses, peas, and beans. However, the phytic acid content in plant proteins—mainly seeds and whole grains—speeds the excretion of zinc. Therefore, if you are a strict vegetarian, you should assess whether your diet is supplying all your zinc requirements.

It is often easy to determine whether you are developing a zinc deficiency. If you have skin problems—wounds that take a long time to heal, white spots on fingernails—or a poor sense of taste or smell, or bad vision in dim light, you are showing the classic signs of zinc deficiency. Any further losses could result in a deterioration of brain function and loss of memory.

If you think you might have a zinc deficiency, you should consult your physician before you change or supplement your diet. Diagnosis and treatment of a medical condition should never be attempted without the advice of your doctor. Prolonged intake of excess zinc can be toxic, and some reports suggest that Pick's disease, a serious brain malfunction, is associated with an excess of zinc in the brain, though it is not clear how this condition is induced.

Vitamins

Vitamins have many different functions, but generally they act as partners with enzymes to promote biochemical reactions. The two major kinds of vitamins are water soluble (B-complex and C) and fat soluble (A, D, E, and K). The water-soluble vitamins are usually found in fresh fruits, vegetables, nuts, whole grain cereals, legumes, and meat and dairy foods. Fat-soluble vitamins are found in enriched margarine (A) or milk (A and D), and in pigmented vegetables such as carrots (A), liver (A), and vegetable seed oils (E). Excess of fat-soluble vitamins can be stored in fat deposits and can accumulate to toxic levels, but excess water-soluble vitamins are usually excreted. By ingesting a varied and complete diet, however, you are not likely to become deficient or to have toxic levels build up. The RDAs for vitamins C (60 milligrams) and B1 (men—1.5 milligrams; women—1.1 milligrams, if pregnant—1.5 milligrams) are easily obtained in a varied and complete diet.

Two of the water-soluble vitamins—thiamine (B1) and ascorbic acid (C)—have received intense scrutiny by brain scientists. Both B1 and C are used by neurons for chemical signaling and the manufacturing of transmitters, and there is exciting new evidence to show that vitamin C may have its own receptors in the areas of the brain that control and coordinate body movements. If this evidence holds up to further scrutiny, it may mean that the simple act of eating an orange can stimulate thousands of your brain's neurons.

EATING FOR YOUR BRAIN

The best way to maintain an adequate flow of nutrients to the brain is to adopt eating habits that enable you to obtain most of those nutrients from your diet. You don't have to balance the three macronutrients—proteins, carbohydrates, and fats—at every meal, and at times you may want to focus on one or more of these nutrients to obtain a specific brain effect. But it is important to ingest foods that build up an adequate sum of nutrients every day or two. Whenever possible, eat fresh raw vegetables and fruits for their vitamin and mineral content. If you are cooking, remember that vitamins and minerals are better retained when you steam vegetables or prepare them in a microwave oven. If you plan to go on a weight-loss diet, I recommend that you choose a complete, balanced diet plan (e.g., Weight Watchers) that allows you to eat adequate amounts of all the nutrients that will feed your brain—and body. Remember, the best protection against large fluctuations in the brain's nutrient supply is to maintain a complete and varied natural diet made of real foods, and not an artificially composed liquid diet.

It is also important to know that some foods we ingest can change our needs for minerals found in other foods. For example, the tannins in a single glass of red wine or cup of tea every night at dinner can seriously decrease your absorption of iron, a trace element important for oxygen exchange in the blood. Moreover, we often get dietary minerals by drinking tap water, but there are regional variations in its mineral content. Thus, if you are feeling sluggish or weak, or you have aching bones, cramps, muscle tremors, or mental fatigue, you should see your physician about whether you need to supplement your diet.

A diet will supply all the known sources of nutrients that are good for your brain if it includes the food groups listed below. (A more detailed discussion of these food groups can be found in *Human Nutrition*, by Benjamin Burton.[11])

MAJOR FOOD GROUPS

Food Group	Nutrient Supply
Meats	
(beef, pork, game, poultry, fish)	high-quality protein, B-vitamins, minerals, trace elements
(liver, other organ meats)	high-quality protein, B-vitamins, vitamin C, vitamin A, minerals, trace elements, choline
Eggs	high-quality protein, vitamins A, B1, and D, choline, minerals, trace elements, easily digested fats
Dairy Products	high-quality protein, calcium, phosphorus (milk fortified with vitamins A, and D), easily digested fats, milk sugar, choline
(milk, cheese, yogurt)	
Cereal Products	low-quality protein, carbohydrate, (vitamins and minerals supplied by enrichment)
(breakfast cereals, breads, noodles)	
Vegetables	carbohydrate, scanty high-quality protein, vitamins A and C, minerals
(potatoes, carrots, beets, turnips)	
(leafy vegetables)	high vitamin and mineral content, scanty high-quality protein, fiber
(peas, beans, peanuts)	rich medium-quality protein, vitamin B1, choline minerals, carbohydrate
(soybeans)	rich high-quality protein, calcium, iron, carbohydrate choline
Nuts	medium-quality protein, fats, vitamin B1, minerals
Fruits	some carbohydrate, vitamins A and C, minerals
(tomatoes)	vitamins A and C, minerals
Fats and Oils	essential fatty acids (vitamins A and D if fortified)
Sugars, Sweets	calories
(dark cane molasses)	calcium, iron

Below are some examples of how to collect these food groups into basic meals. Since the object of these menus is to provide the necessary brain nutrients—not to help you lose weight—I do not include food amounts or calorie sums. Four days of meals are shown to provide examples of variety.

SAMPLE MENUS

	Day 1	Day 2	Day 3	Day 4
B r e a k f a s t	hot cracked wheat or cold whole grain cereal lowfat or skim milk fruit or juice muffin	yogurt and fruit toast or muffin juice	eggs fruit or juice skim milk muffin	"lite" breakfast meat fruit or juice muffin skim milk
L u n c h	boiled shrimp (w/crackers) mixed salad mandarin oranges	chicken sandwich green vegetable mixed fruit dessert	baked potato w/vegetable and yogurt topping mixed fruit dessert	cheese and crackers green vegetables fruit frozen yogurt
D i n n e r	Chinese chicken and vegetables stir-fried in peanut oil mixed salad frozen yogurt w/fruit	boiled crabs mixed salad baked potato mixed fruit	broiled veal brown rice steamed broccoli frozen yogurt w/fruit	lean steak (broiled) boiled new potatoes mixed salad mixed fruit

Specific entries are meant only as examples. You may wish to substitute similar items according to taste (e.g., turkey for chicken or oysters for shrimp). When thirsty, you should drink water or decaffeinated herbal teas. Salads may have a small amount of vege-

table oil as part of a dressing. Muffin/toast can have all-natural pre-
serves. You may wish to avoid the tannins in red wine and tea, which
can decrease absorption of trace elements.

TYING FOOD TO MOOD

Special situations might necessitate some special nutritional strategies to optimize brain function. For that all-important meeting, for
example, you need energy and the basic nutrients for neural transmission, but it also helps to be in a good frame of mind. Though
there are no Dr. Jekyll and Mr. Hyde foods that cause large emotional
swings from depression to cheerfulness (or vice-versa), there are
foods that can give you an emotional edge.

The moods that foods can affect can be divided into two broad
categories: Feelings of alertness, or "up" feelings; and feelings of
relaxation and calm focus.[12] Foods affect these feelings because the
nutrients they contain lead to changes in the levels of the brain's
neural transmitters.

As discussed earlier, neurons in the brain communicate with
each other by releasing little packets of neurotransmitters—substances that convey a specific biochemical meaning when they stimulate other neurons. One class of neurotransmitters, _catecholamines,_
activates the brain to provide feelings of alertness and arousal. These
effects are part of the brain's primitive fight or flight mechanisms to
ensure that all of its survival systems are alert. Anything that elevates
the levels of catecholamines in the brain helps to give you a mental
edge.

Another neurotransmitter, _serotonin,_ acts to release tension,
causing a relaxation response. Experiments with serotonin show that
it has a calming or quieting effect on brain function. Anything that
elevates the levels of brain serotonin thus helps to relax you and
enable you to focus emotionally on important projects—and to develop positive feelings about these projects. If you could eat something that would boost brain serotonin, you could help stimulate this
relaxation response, even if you are under stress at the time.

Fortunately, there are foods that raise the levels of these neurotransmitters in the brain. With the prospect of a high-tension meet-

ing or a critical lecture, you may want to try a dietary approach to handling your frame of mind. There are two basic snack strategies you can use: stimulating or calming. The choice depends on your characteristic responses to the critical situation. If you have trouble focusing or concentrating, you should try snack strategy number 1. If you are feeling a little flat, you should try strategy number 2.

Snack Strategy Number 1—Calming

A relaxation response can be evoked if the diet activates the neurotransmitter serotonin. Serotonin is manufactured from the raw ingredient tryptophan, an essential amino acid found in high-quality protein foods. But eating high-protein foods is not the way to give your brain an immediate shot of tryptophan. This paradoxical situation occurs because tryptophan competes with other amino acids for absorption by the brain. When you eat high-protein foods such as fish or meat, you are taking in several other competing amino acids along with tryptophan. The amounts of tryptophan your brain can use relative to these other amino acids is thus actually lowered.

The best way to give your brain a fast and relaxing shot of tryptophan is to eat foods rich in carbohydrates—starchy or sweet foods. All carbohydrates, whether complex or simple, initiate a chain of physiologic events that begins with an increased release of insulin. The insulin, traveling through your bloodstream, enables tissues (except for the brain) to absorb the competing amino acids. Tryptophan is immune from the insulin action because it is usually bound to another blood-borne substance that protects it. The bloodstream is thus cleaned of the physiologic competitors, and your brain has an easier time absorbing the tryptophan.

Keep in mind that your individual response to a load of carbohydrates may be stronger or weaker than other people's reactions. The baked potato that may give one person a relaxation response could put another to sleep. And a few cookies may be enough for a friend, but it may not make a difference for you. Moreover, you need to know the proper lag time. A dose of carbohydrates can be thought of as a drug, like aspirin. A response to any drug takes different times, depending on when and what your last meal was. The best thing to do, then, is to try a snack of carbohydrates prior to less-critical events. When you find out what gives you the proper relaxation response, and how long it takes to kick in, then you will know what and when to eat before a critical high-tension meeting.

Snack Strategy Number 2—Stimulating

The strategy for an "up" response requires that you eat foods that stimulate the catecholamine neurotransmitters in your brain. Catecholamines are manufactured by enzymes that alter the chemical structure of the amino acid known as tyrosine. Tyrosine is found in high-protein foods: meat, fish, and nuts. When you eat these foods, you are providing your brain with the raw ingredient it needs to make more of its catecholamine neurotransmitters.

The "activated brain" hypothesis is important here, too. The more your brain is actively using catecholamines (when it is performing in situations that require alertness or arousal), the more it takes up tyrosine from the bloodstream. Brain exercises that focus on alertness increase the flow of this nutrient to the brain by making your brain demand more of it. But arousing or stressful situations can also act like brain exercises to increase the nutrient flow of tyrosine.

Other foods that can provide an "up" response include certain cheeses—especially Camembert, Boursault, sharp cheddar, Gruyere, and Stilton—and lox or pickled herring, sauerkraut, figs, raisins, and chocolate. Thus, if you want a slight edge in alertness, try a snack of raisins or figs, or perhaps a chocolate bar. And remember to test your own dose and response time before a critical situation arises, or you may find to your distress that you don't get the mood response you are seeking.

It should be kept in mind that catecholamines also elevate blood pressure. If you are taking any medication at all, whether for a cold or depression, or have problems with high blood pressure, consult a physician before you try a different dietary pattern.

In fact, interactions between food and drugs were first discovered because of a hypertension reaction some depressed patients had after eating cheese. They were being treated with certain antidepressant drugs—MAO inhibitors—that heightened the "up" effect of catecholamines in their brains. No one at the time was aware that certain fermented foods and wines could interact with drugs to cause hypertensive episodes, but the evidence that an amino acid in these foods was responsible soon became clear. Now physicians are aware of this "cheese" story and will routinely warn patients for whom they prescribe this antidepressant drug.

Here is a summary of two basic snack strategies for optimum performance in special situations:

SNACK STRATEGIES

Strategy Number 1: Relaxation Responses	Strategy Number 2: "Up" Responses
Any high-carbohydrate food:	Certain cheeses:
bread	Camembert
crackers	Boursault
muffin	sharp cheddar
potatoes	Gruyere
	Stilton
carrots	
squash	Also:
candy	figs
cookies	raisins
cake	chocolate
apples	nuts or seeds
pears	
bananas	
grapes	

Note that although figs, raisins, and chocolate from group number 2 may have high contents of carbohydrates, they should not be used for the relaxation responses because of their other "up" nutrients. The fruit, vegetables, nuts, and seeds provide significant sources of additional vitamins and minerals for the brain.

With a nutritionally sound diet and knowledge of how to use nutrition to meet your brain's special needs, you are almost ready to prepare your brain biochemically for any intellectual challenge it needs to meet. But you must also be aware of your brain's *other* chemical environment. In the next chapter, we discuss how certain drugs add their effects to the nutritive medium in which neurons live.

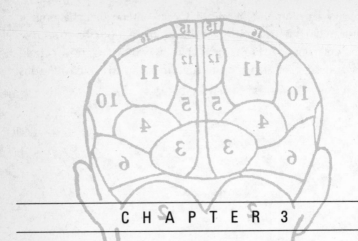

CHAPTER 3

The Brain's Other *Chemical Environment*

The right nutrients have to be available to the brain so that brain exercise can have a beneficial effect, but brain cells need more than a nutritionally complete chemical environment.

As you will recall, neurons signal each other at the synapse via the release of packets of neurochemicals called neurotransmitters. Specific receptors on the receiving end of the neuron decode this chemical signal by recognizing the shape of the particular neurotransmitter used in a neural circuit. This biochemical interaction can be compared to a lock and key, where the receptor is the lock that recognizes only one shape of the neurotransmitter key. However, any one neurotransmitter may have several different receptors which recognize it. Thus, a neurotransmitter is more like a master key for its several receptors.

Various drugs that affect the brain are shaped so much like a neurotransmitter that they can mimic or block the effects of that neurotransmitter at one of its receptors.[1] In fact, the endogenous opiates, known as endorphins, which are neurotransmitters in the brain's pain relief circuits, were discovered only *after* scientists were able to identify that the brain has opiate receptors that recognize morphine. Once the receptors had been discovered, scientists reasoned, it seemed unlikely that the brain would have evolved such a rich concentration of "locks" to fit a set of keys found only in the opium poppy. This "backward" reasoning gave impetus to the idea of "the brain's own morphine" and led to the discovery of endorphins, whose receptor actions were being mimicked by morphine.

When drugs mimic (or block) the effects of neurotransmitters at specific receptors, they can trick the brain into believing it has what it needs, chemically and/or nutritionally, at a time when in fact it does not. To put this in language that may be familiar to you if you are a dieter, certain diet drugs mimic a chemical signal that normally occurs in the brain after you've eaten a meal containing carbohydrates. With these drugs, you feel as satisfied as if you have just eaten a meal, and you find you do not want to eat any more. But your brain only "thinks" that because of the false signals provided by the drug, when in fact the nutrients that normally evoke the satiety signal are not in your system.

Neural plasticity may be similarly affected by outside chemical influences, which is why it is extremely important to avoid drugs that mimic the brain stimulation we'd get through various exercises. Some of these drugs can bring on fatigue, while others will interfere with the positive effects of brain exercise by blocking neurotransmitter reception. Most any change in neurotransmitter reception produced by drugs is the wrong kind of neural change. For example, though certain drugs are administered to stimulate memory in demented patients who lack normal neurotransmitter flow, these drugs can impair strong memories in a brain with normal neurotransmitter flow. Your brain may even undergo what is known as *state dependent learning*, in which what you learn during brain exercise can only be remembered when you are under the influence of the drug.

To give you an idea of how drugs affect brain functioning, I have selected a few representatives of the major drug classes. Many of these drugs also have deleterious effects on other physiological systems—e.g., cocaine on the cardiovascular system, alcohol on the liver, etc.—but these effects lie outside the scope of this book.

SEDATIVE-HYPNOTICS

The class of sedative-hypnotics includes drugs that produce varying degrees of behavioral sedation—alcohol, barbiturates, and antianxiety drugs (Valium), to name a few. The typical neural effect of any particular drug in this class is to depress the neural activity of brain cells. Information flow is reduced as the signaling units begin to slow. The way you feel and act, however, depends on the dosage of the drug. At low doses, nerve circuits that depress behavior are themselves inhibited, producing a state known as *disinhibition* in which behavior may be excited. This is why you may feel a little "loose" or "up" after one drink. Additional amounts of a sedative-hypnotic will produce increasing amounts of sedation, the final result of which (at very high doses) is coma and death. Moreover, the sedation effects of these drugs are additive; the combination of alcohol and Valium, for example, will produce more sedation than a single amount of either drug alone.

Alcohol

A runner wouldn't even consider using alcohol before a race. Muscle cells do not receive the appropriate signals for contraction, nor do they burn energy as efficiently, when they are contracting in a biochemical environment laced with alcohol. Brain cells suffer the same way muscle cells do from the effects of drugs. They cannot receive the appropriate chemical signals for message conduction when alcohol is mixed in the biochemical medium in which they reside.

Alcohol is a depressant that inhibits the normal activities of groups of nerve cells. You may feel enlivened, loosened up, or enhanced in your mental abilities after drinking a small amount of alcohol (one or two beers) but it is a false feeling, simply another example of how a drug can trick a brain. The feeling arises because of the disinhibition mentioned above.

Drinking a glass of wine while you relax at dinner is one thing, but a regimen of brain exercise combined with a three-margarita lunch won't have any beneficial effect. Brain fitness, like any other fitness, depends on cells functioning in a biochemical environment free of substances that impair or artificially enhance neurotransmitter flow.

A considerable body of evidence shows that alcohol can affect your memory. In one scientific study,[2] adult volunteers who were treated with low or high doses of alcohol were impaired in their recall of a list of words that had not been well practiced and were therefore poorly learned. High doses impaired memory more than low doses, but even the low alcohol doses had a significant effect. Alcohol seems to interfere with the ability to process and store new information, and there is even some evidence that it impairs the memory of women more than it does that of men. Whether this is because the sexes absorb and eliminate alcohol at different rates is not clear. However, whatever your sex, if you have to remember what your client says at lunch, it is wise to pass on the margaritas.

STIMULANTS

The drugs that stimulate nervous system activity do not comprise a homogeneous class, because they affect different receptors in the brain. Both caffeine and nicotine stimulate neurons, but they do so in radically different ways: Caffeine acts within a neuron to stimulate its metabolism, while nicotine stimulates the "nicotinic" receptors of the neurotransmitter acetylcholine. Behavioral stimulants, on the other hand, usually elevate information flow in the neurotransmitter norepinephrine, but they may do so in different ways, with different effects. Both cocaine and amphetamines can be included in this subcategory. There are also the clinical antidepressants that alter the flow of norepinephrine, as well as other neurotransmitters. Moreover, many of the decongestants and other cold remedies have some stimulant actions on the central nervous system.

Cocaine

Cocaine is a psychoactive drug—that is, a substance that is actively absorbed into brain cells where it has a direct effect on neural communication. During normal brain function, information flow is achieved when neurons release neurotransmitters, which, by interacting with receptors, stimulate or inhibit the cells with which they connect. Neurotransmitters, once released, are then removed from the synapse by metabolic enzymes and an "uptake" mechanism, by which the releasing fibers reabsorb the neurotransmitters. Cocaine can inhibit this uptake mechanism, preventing nerves from reabsorbing the transmitters they released. More neurotransmitters are then available to stimulate (or inhibit) the connecting cells.

Cocaine inhibits the uptake mechanism primarily in the neurons that release dopamine as a neurotransmitter. The extra dopamine available to interact with its receptors induces euphoria and increases alertness, giving the user an overall feeling of pleasure. If the action of dopamine is prolonged by higher or additional doses, the pleasurable reaction may give way to irritability or paranoia.

If the brain was not able to react so vigorously to this distorted information flow, the use of cocaine might not be so damaging. However, as information flow increases in any neurotransmitter system, feedback mechanisms in the connecting cells act to limit the distorted flow by decreasing the number of receptors for the neurotransmitter. This mechanism is analogous to the way you would adjust the water controls in a dormitory or locker room shower to maintain a constant temperature. If the water suddenly became too cold, you would have to "down-regulate" (the term used for receptors) the cold water control until the temperature became optimal again. Unfortunately, as the connecting cell down-regulates its receptors for dopamine, it takes more and more of a neurotransmitter rush to achieve the same level of euphoria. This decreased responsiveness to a drug is known as tolerance, a process which can lead to a desire for more and more cocaine to achieve the same effect. Moreover, drugs like cocaine that produce such a pleasurable feeling can lead to dependence, a state in which your mind "concludes" that it cannot do without the drug to function normally.

Amphetamines

The chemical structure of amphetamines (e.g., Dexedrine, Bipheta-mine) is quite close to that of the neurotransmitters dopamine and norepinephrine. Amphetamines not only act in the brain to release these transmitters, but they are similar enough to stimulate their receptors. The alertness and arousal one feels under the influence of an amphetamine is due to these neural actions. However, as with cocaine, brain cells "adapt" to the distorted information flow, pro-ducing a tolerance in which more and more of the drug is required to achieve the same feeling. A dependence on amphetamines can also develop, because its effects are pleasurable. As dependence builds, and the increasing tolerance demands larger and larger doses of the drug, the user can develop an extreme paranoid state known as amphetamine psychosis.

Caffeine

It is difficult to find a person who has never had some caffeine, a stimulant found in significant levels in coffee, tea, cola drinks, and chocolate. Caffeine produces feelings of alertness and well-being, but not by increasing the neurotransmitter flow like the other stim-ulants we have discussed. Instead, caffeine acts on a "second mes-senger" process inside a nerve cell after its receptors have been stimulated by a neurotransmitter. Certain receptors signal the nu-cleus of a nerve by generating a "second messenger" known as cyclic AMP. Like other biochemicals used for signaling, cyclic AMP is deac-tivated by an enzyme, thereby turning off the signal after the cell nucleus has received it. Caffeine inhibits this enzyme, thus allowing cyclic AMP a longer time to have its second messenger effect.

Some tolerance will develop to caffeine, especially if ingested in large quantities or in direct stimulant form (tablets) as an alertness aid for long distance night driving. Caffeine may also create a minor dependence, as those of you who need a cup of coffee after a meal will attest. The dependence may also be perceived if you quit caffeine "cold turkey" and begin to feel like you have the flu.

Normally, a couple of cups of coffee during the day will not significantly interfere with information flow in the brain. Moderation is the key. If you have developed a tolerance to higher "doses" of caffeine you are risking the downside effects of stimulant overuse —irritability, sleeplessness, fatigue—all of which may interfere with your ability to benefit from brain exercise.

Nicotine

The active ingredient in tobacco, nicotine, achieves its stimulant and relaxation properties by acting on receptors of the neurotransmitter acetylcholine. Some of nicotine's stimulant properties may be traceable to its ability to release adrenaline from the adrenal gland.

Chronic users of nicotine may develop tolerance and require more of the drug to achieve the same pleasurable effects. Dependence on these effects can be quite strong and may make it very difficult to give up smoking.

Small amounts of nicotine by itself will not seriously interfere with information flow in the brain. However, smoking also introduces significant amounts of carbon monoxide into the bloodstream, which will decrease the amount of oxygen delivered to the brain. Thus, even ignoring the cancer risk and other smoking-related health problems that can decrease brain functioning, you will, by smoking, reduce the effectiveness of brain exercise.

Marijuana

The principal ingredient thought to be responsible for marijuana's pleasant effects, delta9-tetrahydrocannabinol (δ9-THC), is difficult to classify. It is not a sedative-hypnotic, though it can potentiate the behavioral depressant effects of alcohol or barbiturates. It is also not a stimulant, though it promotes feelings of euphoria, or increased well-being. Marijuana can also heighten one's perception of the sensory qualities of objects or events, such that things previously unnoticed in the background may take on new and appealing qualities. Users also report an altered perception of time and cravings for foods. Higher doses may result in strong hallucinations and can lead to attacks of anxiety, paranoia, or delusions.

Although marijuana use is generally pleasurable, it is not recommended for optimal brain functioning. As with tobacco, its use is associated with increased carbon monoxide, which can deprive the brain of oxygen. Chronic use can even lead to apathy, mental dullness, and loss of concentration.

PRESCRIPTION AND OVER-THE-COUNTER REMEDIES

While it would not be advisable to give up antidepressants, antianxiety drugs, or pain medication for the purpose of brain exercise, some thought should be given to the effects of these drugs on brain function. Also, though symptomatic relief for a cold may alter neurotransmitter flow to some extent, the effect may be preferable to the drag on mental functions caused by the cold in the first place. Moreover, different cold remedies have different effects on the brain and their side effects are listed on the package. You should have enough information (from past experiences with products and product information) to be able to choose.

Prescription Drugs

Antidepressants have more specific but similar effects on the brain as cocaine; however, they do not give the immediate uplifting euphoric effect of cocaine. One of the widely used antidepressants, Prozac, a form of fluoxetine, decreases the uptake of the neurotransmitter serotonin. Information flow in serotonin neural circuits is increased, but there are no major changes in mental abilities. In fact, Prozac requires several days to take effect on the depressed condition, at which time the patient feels an uplifting of spirit but no other changes in thinking or reasoning ability. The drug thus seems to be rather selective for the depressed condition, and, if prescribed, can be a welcome relief from the drag on mental functions caused by the condition.

Antianxiety drugs such as Valium, the chemical name for which is diazepam, can be considered as sedative-hypnotics, though they are much more specific in their actions on the nervous system than alcohol or barbiturates. These antianxiety drugs are prescribed for anxiety and tension, but excessive use may produce confusion and impaired memory. If prescribed, they can be a welcome relief from the anxiety that is impairing one's ability to concentrate.

Opiate narcotics such as morphine relieve pain by stimulating receptors for naturally occurring opiates in the brain. The receptor stimulation seems to remove the emotional awareness of the pain without taking away the sensory experience of the wound; you know it still hurts, but you no longer care. Opiates usually induce drowsiness and mental clouding, though some patients may experience agitation. Positive effects of brain exercise will likely not be achieved to their full extent if you are being treated with opiates; in this case it would be best to wait until treatment is complete.

Over-the-Counter Drugs

Like all neurotransmitters (e.g., serotonin, norepinephrine), histamine is released from nerve terminals, where it then has a signaling effect on nerve cells that have histamine receptors. Antihistamines, by blocking the receptors, prevent histamines from achieving their normal neural signaling.

Though antihistamines are taken as decongestants, in the brain they have the side effect of preventing the reception of signals that affect mental alertness and arousal. When you take antihistamines, you become drowsy because of the blocking of these alertness signals. Antihistamines such as pheniramine or chlorpheniramine, available in many over-the-counter preparations, are quite effective as decongestants, but they can prevent your brain from responding to the stimulation produced by normal interactions with the environment, not to mention brain exercise.

The drug phenylpropanolamine, initially used as a nasal decongestant, was discovered to have an interesting side effect: It caused people to lose weight. Since that discovery, phenylpropanolamine has been marketed as both a decongestant and a diet aid in many popular remedies, and is readily available without a prescription.

Although phenylpropanolamine has less of an effect on the brain, there are receptors in the brain that respond to this drug. In fact, the antihunger effect of phenylpropanolamine may come about through its action on a primitive part of the brain called the hypo-thalamus. Behaviorally, this drug could be classed as a mild stimulant; it causes a slight "up" or aroused feeling.

Pseudoephedrine, another popular decongestant found in Su-dafed and other cold remedies, is also a mild stimulant, though most of its receptor stimulation occurs not in the brain but in the bronchial airways. Both of these decongestants—pseudoephedrine and phenylpropanolamine—permit you the freedom when you have a cold to exercise your brain without drowsiness by stimulating the brain only slightly.

TOXINS IN THE BRAIN'S CHEMICAL ENVIRONMENT

The ideal chemical environment for a brain is not only well stocked with essential nutrients but free of the abnormal signals produced by drugs. It should also be free of toxins that destroy its ability to carry on normal neural processes.

A toxin is similar to a drug, except that it is less specific in its actions. Toxins affect brain cells and alter their neural adaptive pro-cesses as drugs do, but the effects of toxins are usually more wide-spread. In fact, many toxins can affect the entire brain, virtually shutting down all normal thought processes.

Aluminum

The use of aluminum in cooking, storage, condiment preparation, antacids, and deodorants is on the rise, despite the evidence that aluminum is involved in brain disease. Aluminum in the chemical environment has been linked to several forms of nerve disorders, including Alzheimer's disease. Although the evidence is not conclu-sive, it does show that aluminum can be deleterious to the health of brain tissue.

Alzheimer's disease is a disorder of the nervous system in which the proteins of certain brain cells twist together and form fibrous tangles. These tangles take up a lot of space within nerve cells and choke off their normal signaling functions. One medical report I examined[3] shows that 91 percent of the brain cells that contain tangles in an Alzheimer's patient are contaminated with aluminum. Only 4 percent of the brain cells without the tangles have aluminum. With statistics such as these, it is hard to think of the presence of aluminum in these degenerate nerve cells as a coincidence.

Other bits and pieces of evidence also implicate aluminum as a brain toxin. The brains of patients who undergo intellectual deterioration after blood dialysis have abnormally high concentrations of aluminum. And research on natives of Guam indicates an unnaturally high incidence of nerve degeneration. After autopsy, the brains of these people show elevated levels of aluminum and the degenerate brain cells that have fibrous protein tangles. Moreover, a report in the medical journal *Lancet* indicates a geographic relationship between Alzheimer's disease and aluminum in drinking water.[4] In this study, the risk of Alzheimer's disease was 1.5 times higher in districts where the average aluminum concentration exceeded 0.11 milligrams per liter than in districts where the concentrations were less than 0.01 milligrams per liter.

Still, no one knows for sure why some people are more sensitive than others to the effects of aluminum, or even whether dietary aluminum is an actual cause of brain malfunction. The only thing we can say for certain is that aluminum is linked to harmful brain effects and that people generally feel better when they decrease their contact with aluminum.

Are you absorbing aluminum without knowing it? Here are some of the ways you may be getting it: Wrapping acidic foods such as cut tomatoes or lemons in aluminum foil, cooking acidic foods in aluminum pots or scraping an aluminum pot with a metal utensil while food is cooking, and taking popular antacids for an upset stomach (check the ingredients to see if your antacid contains aluminum). Moreover, deposits in environmental groundwater and acid rain reduce the soil's ability to keep aluminum from draining, thus allowing aluminum to get into the food chain. Aluminum silicate compounds are used to keep table salts and condiments free-flowing, and aluminum antiwetness compounds are applied daily to the skin in deodorants.

Look around you and read all the labels. Try to eliminate aluminum from your dietary environment. Even if the evidence is not conclusive, you owe it to your brain to keep it free from potentially harmful substances. And because of its association with degeneration of brain tissue and function, aluminum is one of the substances you might want to go out of your way to avoid.

Other Toxic Metals

In small amounts, metals such as zinc, iron, and copper are essential to health and well-being. These metals, especially zinc, are found in neurons of the brain where they participate in important biochemical reactions that control neural signaling, the manufacturing of neurotransmitters, and the receptive properties of nerve membranes.

Even small amounts of nickel and chromium taken in the diet are useful in biochemical reactions. Though their importance in brain function is less well known, their absence is noted when it becomes harder to carry out mental tasks because you feel run down and mentally fatigued. Other metals like cadmium, mercury, and lead have little or no biological value. You would never miss them if you could exclude them from the environment, yet if they are taken into the body, they eventually find their way to the brain and have a negative effect on brain performance.

You generally have no trouble acquiring beneficial trace metals if you eat a complete and varied diet. But you are also likely to have the opposite problem. Environmental pollutants that include auto exhaust, tobacco smoke, and industrial emissions often force you to breathe in unacceptable levels of toxic metals. Short of dropping out of life, there is really no good way to avoid some contamination with toxic metals.

So what can you do to protect your brain?[5] The best protection against brain contamination is to make sure you get enough of the beneficial vitamins and minerals: calcium, zinc, iron, selenium, and vitamin C. When the toxic metals are ingested or inhaled, they usually have to compete with the metals that have biological or nutritional value. Toxic metals especially infiltrate areas of the brain like the hippocampus, which normally use biological metals such as zinc, iron, and calcium for the neural communication of memory and spatial ability. If you are lacking in zinc, iron, or calcium, the toxic metals can build up and cause memory problems and loss of spatial ability. If you keep yourself fortified with the biological metals and minerals (zinc, iron, calcium), you can protect your brain.

The brain needs three basic chemical conditions to be able to increase its abilities through exercise. First, it needs a strong nutritional base so that exercise can lead to appropriate kinds of neural adaptation. Second, it needs to be relatively free of drugs that can alter the course of normal neural adaptation. Third, it needs to be as free of toxic substances as possible. Given these chemical conditions, you can maximize the benefits of brain exercise. But first, before the exercises, you will need to tone up your brain. The next chapter focuses on general brain fitness.

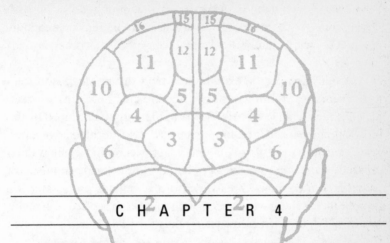

CHAPTER 4

Toning Up Your Brain

I t is hard enough to exercise a brain that lacks an adequate chemical environment, but it is virtually impossible to exercise a tired brain. Attention and focusing ability suffer when your brain is tired. These are the mechanisms that allow brain exercise to gain access to nerve cells. With a tired brain, you can exercise as much as you want, but the information won't reach the brain neurons where it will do the most good. Four factors are critical in keeping your brain refreshed and ready for exercise: sleep, enjoyment, physical fitness, and prevention of fatigue.

SLEEP: THE MEMORY BOOSTER

We used to think of sleep as a period of rest that allowed the brain (and other organs) to recover from the "wear and tear" of daily life.

We now know that the brain does not rest during sleep—at least not all of it. On the contrary, electrical activity, oxygen consumption, and energy expenditure in certain regions of the brain actually increase.

One purpose of the extra brain activity during sleep is to reinforce memories.[1] During this extra neural activity, proteins are manufactured by nerve cells. These proteins, like those produced by the stimulation from directed brain exercise, help store cellular memories. It is important that you get enough sleep time to allow such protein production to occur because part of the "wear and tear" of daily life is a continual breakdown of the cellular proteins. If the proteins in the brain were to decay without being replaced, all memory would gradually be lost. Sleep thus serves to retain memories (or memory fragments) through protein replacement which counteracts the continual wear and tear.

Sleep not only aids in retaining cellular memories, but it helps us sort out the load of recent information we have acquired during the day. Everything we see, hear, smell, taste, or touch bombards us with an immense wealth of information. Even the simple act of reading this book channels more information into the brain than can be handled by the average desktop computer. This is because the "information" the brain "sees" is composed of much more than the meanings of the words on the page: It includes the size and shape of words, the space between the lines, the feel of the book, the contrast between the book and the background objects scattered on the desk or in the room, and a myriad of other bits and pieces too subtle to name.

Events that we wish to remember are amalgamations of so much detail that we could never "cram it all in" without a good means of reorganization. Sleep provides the brain with a way to shuffle this excess information into a convenient plan of neural storage. Without sleep, our memories would be smaller.

Sleep can be likened to a file clerk who always finds ways to get new information (files) in, even if some of it has to be combined with old information. Without sleep, we lose much of our ability to transfer the day's information into long-term memories. Losing sleep is like firing the file clerk and having to make do without anyone to help with the reorganization of the important daily information.

I often take a catnap about one or two o'clock in the afternoon. This is a time after I have done my morning's writing, and my brain is swimming with facts. A ten- or fifteen-minute "blank out" is enough to charge me up for the rest of the afternoon. Even if the nap leaves me physically out of touch for a while, my mind is sharper and more capable of redirecting my writing efforts. This way I have two "mornings" of sharp mental activity in a day.

If you have a job in which a catnap may be inappropriate or impractical, all is not lost. That's because you may not need to actually "blank out" to get many of the benefits of an afternoon nap.[2] A period of quiet time away from the normal influx of information will allow your brain to do some of the filing necessary to sharpen your memory. A crossword puzzle, a good novel, a brief meditation or guided relaxation exercise—anything that stops the normal flow and lets your brain redirect—is worthwhile. Anthropologists Marsha Thompson and David Harsha have shown that the time your brain most needs this redirection varies with your individual daily biological clock. This is usually the time of the day when you feel most sleepy. And you shouldn't try to fight it with increased activity or an extra cup of coffee. Your brain is trying to tell you something.

A few simple guidelines are effective if you have trouble getting to sleep at night. First, evaluate your caffeine intake. A cup of coffee after dinner or late at night is a serious offender. Continual consumption of caffeine during the day can also build up levels that your body may not have time to remove by bedtime. Reducing—or better yet removing—caffeine from your life can work wonders. I speak from experience: My mind no longer races at bedtime, and I drop right off. Moreover, during the day, I feel generally calmer. It surprised me to learn how much of an effect caffeine had been having on me. I did not have to give up chocolate, and with all the decaffeinated coffees, I can even have an espresso after dinner.

Another thing to avoid if you're having trouble sleeping is the consumption of high-protein foods shortly before going to bed. Once the proteins break down, they release amino acids that compete with the amino acid tryptophan for entry into the brain. By competing with tryptophan and preventing its entry into the brain, the high-protein amino acids rob you of a natural brain relaxation process, because tryptophan is converted by the brain into the neural transmitter serotonin, which relaxes you and helps you get to sleep.[3]

Pure tryptophan can no longer be purchased in tablet form in any health food store or pharmacy because it has been implicated in a rare blood disease. This is unfortunate, because it was far better as a sleep aid than the standard drugs that induce drowsiness. These drugs deprive you of the rapid eye movement (REM) stage of sleep that is most important for the filing of daily experience. In fact, if you are deprived of this one sleep stage, but allowed to sleep during other stages, you will be more tired and irritable than if you had stayed up half the night. Tryptophan, by its conversion into a natural brain chemical, aids in achieving a natural sleep in which you are not deprived of the critical REM stage.

If you want to try an even more natural sleep aid that does not involve taking a tablet, try eating a high-carbohydrate food about half an hour before bedtime. Some toast and jam, or a few crackers, will give you enough carbohydrate to set off the insulin response that increases the brain's absorption of tryptophan. You should feel as ready for sleep as if you had taken a tryptophan tablet. If you have eliminated caffeine from your diet, avoided heavy protein meats before bedtime, dosed yourself with a small carbohydrate snack, and you still can't get to sleep, you owe it to yourself to take your insomnia to a therapist.

ENJOYMENT: ITS OWN REWARD—AND MORE

I cannot pronounce the name of the fellow who is probably the world's top expert on enjoyment, but I get the impression that Mihaly Csikszentmihalyi, professor at the Department of Human Development and Education at the University of Chicago, would not mind too much. Presumably he's "going with the flow," and he would probably counsel me to do likewise.

Enjoyment makes life worth living. It helps us feel better about ourselves, and it enables us to learn more from our experiences.

Csikszentmihalyi has studied hundreds of people—artists, athletes, chess players, dancers, rock climbers—who were interviewed about how they feel when they are doing what they enjoy. Their descriptions of enjoyment were so similar, no matter how different the activity, that Csikszentmihalyi calls all such heightened forms of experience "flow states" or "flow experiences."[4]

"Flow states" are what the scientist at work in his lab, the artist who is painting, the runner in the marathon, even the burglar at the moment of crime, all have in common when they are completely absorbed by what they are doing. During a flow experience, you often cease to be aware of anything outside the activity in which you are engaged. Self-consciousness and self-doubt disappear, and you are likely to lose all awareness of time. The flow experience is exciting and fulfilling, a reward unto itself. But the flow experience has ramifications that go beyond mere pleasure; it expands your potential by its effects on the brain.

It's important to create rewarding experiences for yourself, to have an enjoyable atmosphere in which to engage in mental activities. As psychology professor Alice Isen of the University of Maryland has found,[5] people are more innovative about problem-solving if they feel good. Whatever it takes to put you in a good mood—even something as simple as listening to a funny joke—works to your benefit. You will improve your effectiveness, even under surprising or trying conditions. Feeling good helps us to concentrate our attention and persevere at tasks, because enjoyment has specific physiological effects on our brains. Whether we choose to enjoy ourselves by sitting back and listening to our favorite music, taking a couple of sky dives, or going back into the lab to continue work on that all-absorbing problem we feel on the verge of solving, our brains release internal opiates and other neurotransmitters that create our feelings of pleasure. And while the pleasure is being created, memories of the skills that brought us that pleasure are being established. Computer imaging studies show that when we are being rewarded our brains increase the intake of oxygen and nutrients, which of course enhances brain function.

Any mental activity that "feels good" to you is a "reward" and will induce positive changes in the brain, ranging from the release of natural opiates to the consumption of more brain-enhancing oxygen and nutrients. The memories created by these plastic neural changes make it easier for you to engage in that mental activity the next time you attempt it. Thus, the brain exercises that "feel good" to you will enable you to elevate your level of mental activity. Though a large menu of brain exercises will be offered, no one can tell you which ones you *should* choose; what gives you pleasure—and its rewards—will be individual to you. The amount you will learn from brain exercise is therefore completely up to you.

Since only you can decide what is rewarding to your brain, only you will know which of the several games and puzzles in each brain exercise category described in the following chapters are best for you (i.e., most rewarding). I will provide you with a basic game plan, and you can pick and choose among the brain exercises at will, but a really rewarding game usually chooses you. If you happen to find other more rewarding games or puzzles from other sources, then by all means use those. You derive intellectual power and brain fitness only when you feel rewarded by the brain exercise you've performed.

Keep in mind that the value of a reward depends on what you expect. The identical paycheck will seem larger if it represents a raise, smaller if it is a cut in salary. Your approach to any brain exercise is therefore most important in determining the value you will derive from it. If you are too ambitious, you can rapidly lose the reward value of an exercise because you may be expecting a lot more than you could possibly get. If you go into it without any enthusiasm or sense of expectation, on the other hand, you are also likely not to experience any reward value, hence not to enjoy any of the possible neural benefits.

It is therefore important to approach any brain exercise as a flow experience, not a test. You want the exercises to grab and keep your attention, to focus you in the moment, to be intrinsically pleasurable—which will result in an extra charge of oxygen and nutrients to the brain. The only valuable brain exercises are the rewarding ones.

This is not to say you shouldn't measure your performance. Improvement is often faster when you know where you start and what your level is after practice. Improvement should be measured, but measuring shouldn't interfere with pleasure, even if the results aren't as dramatic as you had hoped. Have some fun: Improvement will eventually come naturally as a result.

PHYSICAL FITNESS: ANOTHER FORM OF BRAIN FITNESS

We have all been inundated with information about keeping our bodies fit. You already know that exercise strengthens muscle and cardiovascular tone, improves your body's abilities to use nutrients and oxygen, and makes you look great. You also know that exercise increases your resistance to fatigue and enables you to carry on daily life with a much higher rate of performance. By making your body fit, you encounter fewer health problems and can live a more vigorous life.

While we all know about the physical effects of exercising our bodies, few of us stop to consider what mediates those effects—the brain. But in fact when you stop to think about it, it's obvious, because one of the brain's biggest functions is to coordinate your movements through the physical world.

When you exercise any mental function, the brain cells that control that function become active and develop cellular memories of the exercise; they are adapting to it. As this neural adaptation proceeds, your brain gets better at controlling those functions. If you are engaging in a physical activity—i.e., a tennis stroke—the brain cells which control that movement are doing the adapting. As a result, your timing and coordination of that movement improves. If you've ever learned to play the piano, dance, ride a horse, sew, or play tennis—anything that requires coordinated movement—you've noticed that your performance got better with practice. Your movements became quicker and less prone to error.

The basis for your improvement, however, wasn't in your muscles, as you might have thought, but in your brain. As the relevant nerve cells developed their adaptive memories of your physical exercise, the movements they control became more fluent and decisive. Obviously, then, the more activities you are willing to try to learn to do, the more you will increase the neural adaptation of larger numbers of brain cells.

As if this weren't enough, consider that most of the brain's systems communicate with each other—either through direct nerve fiber contact or via other intermediary nerve pathways. When you exercise one brain system, it will communicate that exercise through those nerve pathways to several other interrelated systems. Physical exercise thus builds not only its own neuronal adaptation, enabling you to get better at the specific activity in which you are engaging, but it also stimulates the plasticity of brain cells in connected brain systems. By exercising all your brain functions, even the physical ones, you build a greater neural base that you can call on for a wide range of uses in the future.

Latent Learning

A fit brain can do strange and wonderful things. Once you have performed a physical exercise often enough that your brain has had the experience of engaging in a fluent and virtually errorless version of it, you can develop a new way of rehearsing it—mentally instead of physically. This is the concept of "psychocybernetics."

My father introduced me to Maxwell Maltz's *Psycho-Cybernetics and Self-Fulfillment*[6] when I was in junior high school. At the time my gym class was doing a section on basketball, and we were being graded on free-throw style, so I thought I'd give Maltz's theories a try. The night before the test, I practiced imagining my free throws. I could see myself in my mind's eye stepping up to the line, aiming the ball, and giving it a perfect arch into the basket. And that is exactly what happened the next day when I was graded on it.

I used the same technique when I was in high school and played a tennis match with a superior player. I knew how to play the game, and I practiced frequently on the court, but every night during the week before the match I added mental exercise to my physical regimen, imagining myself playing every kind of shot. I envisioned playing the game of my life—and I did. Though my opponent was still superior and eventually beat me, I stretched him out an extra set and made him work for every point.

Imagining is frequently used in the brain exercises you will be performing. Some behaviors can be enhanced without actual physical rehearsal of them. Psychologists call it "latent learning," when you learn without actually doing. The process works because to imagine yourself performing a physical activity you must stimulate the brain cells that control that activity.

FATIGUE: YOUR BRAIN GETS TIRED

Muscle fatigue takes place for at least two reasons: Either the nerves that transmit commands to and from the muscles get tired, or the muscle fibers themselves begin to fatigue—or both. Nerve and muscle cells alike become tired when they can no longer acquire energy or nutrients fast enough to continue performing at their present level of activity.

We all know what muscle fatigue feels like, but we may not have thought about mental fatigue as having a similar basis in physiology. Make no mistake—it does. The transmission of nerve messages—to the muscles or within the brain—involves the rapid exchange of charged particles (ions) obtained from eating foods with sodium (salt), potassium, and calcium. The nerve message itself is a chemo-electric impulse, not unlike that from a battery. And neural batteries get recharged from the chemical energy in foods.

Say that you are worrying an idea to death. If you belabor a problem, the brain cells handling it undergo concentrated activity. This means they will rapidly exchange ions between their inner compartments and the brain's fluids. It takes energy to recharge all those ions. If brain cells conduct too many messages in too short a period of time, they will exchange so many ions that they can no longer recover easily. These nerves are now fatigued and will have trouble sending out messages again until they can recover. Your brain will feel limp after an intense mental effort. You know the symptoms: Decreased pleasure from the effort, irritability, inability to concentrate or attend to the problem, mental slowness, and an increased number of mistakes.

It is easy to become more aware of brain fatigue. Your reaction times will increase until you notice you are not so quick on the uptake. Things people tell you do not "click" as readily. Problem-solving time increases: You cannot work out that timetable as easily as usual. Errors increase: You go down more culs-de-sac in solving a problem. In short, your judgment is not as fine as it normally is.

Brain fatigue means that your brain is no longer ready to take in information. It is shutting down, and trying desperately to let you know how it feels. You need to listen to what your brain is telling you about its readiness to perform.

Steady progress in brain improvement can be likened to company profits during a period of economic growth or to stock prices during a bull market. You are likely to see a jagged line with a generally upward trend. "Corrections" occur on some days when conditions are not right, and you have a brief downturn. "Plateaus" occur during some periods when you have all the growth you are going to get for a while and are awaiting the next upturn. Corrections and plateaus do not mean lack of progress, because the general upward trend is still there. You simply have to understand that the occasional glitches are going to occur.

As you exercise your brain, there will be periods when you don't improve. Some days your brain will take a downturn. Fatigue will sometimes occur *during* the brain exercise; even a day on which you improve can be marked by a downturn toward the end of exercise. But this is natural, so don't be discouraged. As you learn to monitor your brain, you will develop a sensitivity to what and how much you can do during periods of brain exercise.

Watch out for overdoing it. A muscle cramps when it can no longer exchange ions. And while we don't know what the precise mental equivalent is, for purposes of this book you can think of "brain cramp" as a glitch in mental performance. It could be forgetting the vice president's name, losing your set of keys, being unable to process what your colleague is telling you about a statistical projection—or even blowing up irrationally at your secretary. You can learn to avoid "brain cramp" as you learn to monitor your fatigue.

Sleep, reward, physical exercise, and prevention of fatigue: These are the critical constituents of brain fitness. They enable your brain to perform at its peak and help your brain improve through exercise. If you fall behind on even one of these factors, it may be difficult to improve your performance. It would be like expecting a smooth-running corporation to make do without its marketing department. It can't be done. You must have all your departments running at high efficiency if the corporation is to grow. The same is true of your brain.

PART TWO

Exercising the Brain

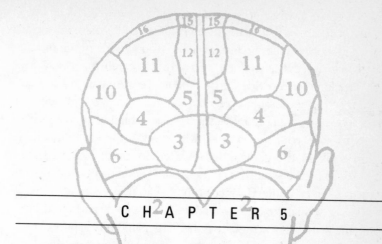

C H A P T E R 5

Exercising Your Brain's Spatial Abilities

Before you ever begin exercising your innate linguistic capacity, you are making use of your spatial abilities, for you are born needing to locate food and other important objects (like Mom or Dad) in your environment. Early in life, you begin to store the collection of spatial features that make up your parents' faces. Your brain can easily tell when strangers' faces do not match this spatial memory. You also begin to manipulate objects in your little world. You learn to reach out and find the toys that dance and float in front of you on the mobile over the crib. Your pacifier gets away from you, and you learn to find and retrieve it.

By seeing, touching, hearing, and smelling, you begin to piece together a world. Before you are nine to ten months old (on average), if a toy rolls out of sight underneath a sofa, that toy is truly out of mind. Your nascent spatial abilities cannot handle the concept that objects exist when they are out of sight. At about nine or ten months, when this concept is attained, you actively search for absent toys, thus providing clear evidence of a mental representation—a spatial memory—of the missing object. At age two, if one of two identical glasses of milk is poured into a short, squat container so that its level *appears* lower, your spatial sense will lead you to believe that there is less milk in the container. However, four-year-olds judge the amounts to be the same; they have become able to conceptualize an objective spatial reality distinct from appearances.

Other spatial concepts are added as you grow and learn more about the world. As you piece together larger amounts of information, you begin to develop greater abilities of abstraction. You develop a *mind's eye* and can decide, for example, how clothing will look on you before you try it on, or how the new office furniture you have just ordered should be arranged for maximum efficiency as well as aesthetic appeal. You develop an appreciation for interesting spatial forms and respond to the manipulation of space that is a very essential part of the beauty in visual art.

YOUR SPATIAL INTELLIGENCE

Spatial functions are of such importance to our mental abilities that psychologists routinely examine them on intelligence tests. For example, the revised Wechsler Adult Intelligence Scale includes at least four tests of spatial abilities: picture completion, picture arrangement, block design, and object assembly, scores for which are included in the overall assessment of your intelligence level.

The picture completion test is much like the adult version of those picture puzzles we played with as children. You are shown a series of cards, each containing a picture with an important element missing. The picture may be of a tennis game without a ball; a person with only one eyebrow; a cat that has no tail. You are allowed twenty seconds to find the missing part, and you get a point for each correct "find."

In the picture arrangement test, you are presented with several series of pictures, but each series is out of order. For example, one set of pictures might show a person preparing dinner. The pictures would portray the various stages of preparation—assembling all the ingredients, mixing them, placing the results in the oven, then removing and serving the meal—but the order of all those steps would be scrambled. Your ability to order the series is timed. You get a point for each series you order correctly and you get additional points for speed.

For the block design test, you assemble blocks—like children's playing blocks—to match the examiner's design. The blocks have two sides—two white sides and two half red and half white sides. You are timed, and you get bonus points for especially fast times. This test requires little cultural knowledge, but it helps if you have practiced playing with blocks and shapes. Playing with a Rubik's cube would be a good way to stimulate performance.

The object assembly test is essentially a simple jigsaw puzzle in which you are timed and given points for speed and accuracy of performance. You are given partial credit for partial completion. For example, one puzzle might be shaped like a giraffe, and you would have to join eight jigsaw pieces together.

As you can tell, test performance is in part dependent on the amount of cultural knowledge the test taker shares with the test maker. For example, you have to know something about tennis to know that the game requires a ball, and you have to have seen cats to know that they have tails. Since knowledge is based on memories, those people who have not had the cultural contact to build the necessary memories will not perform well on this test—regardless of how intelligent they are.

I am not trying to attack intelligence tests so much as to point out that neuronal memories—which are so crucial a factor in intelligence scores—can be expanded through experience. Although it is debatable whether you can actually increase your intelligence, you *can* increase your spatial abilities; hence, your score on intelligence tests. But the real advantage is that you will have enhanced your ability to perform whatever spatial tasks confront you in daily life.

YOUR BRAIN'S SENSE OF SPACE

Our language and culture are studded with examples of how difficult it is to translate spatial thoughts into verbal terms. A picture is worth a thousand words, and it is nearly impossible to describe verbally all the details contained in a dream, or even a single photograph. The classic example is to ask someone to describe a spiral staircase. The response time will be slow, and when your friend finds out that there are few words for it in her brain's verbal storehouse, she will usually end up making an upward spiraling gesture with a finger.

Spatial abilities are controlled by the brain, but because it is difficult to describe what they are, it is hard for scientists to find out how our brains control them. We do know that our brains are not built with specific circuits for specific spatial abilities; it is more subtle than that. We also know that, for the most part, verbal and spatial abilities are controlled by opposite halves of the brain—hence our difficulty in using words to describe our spatial concepts. Beyond these two "rules" of brain organization, we are only beginning to glimpse the ways our brains handle space. However, these glimpses provide us with tools to select and vary the stimulation of the brain's diverse spatial functions.

Focusing on the Sights

The ability of the brain to focus on specific features of the visible environment is called *visual attention*. It is this ability that allows our brains to select those objects we wish to attend to, while ignoring irrelevant background images. The comparable function for skin sensation is the ability to ignore the constant rub and pressure of our clothes while we react immediately to the touch of something sharp or hot. Visual attention is the ability to focus on the image of a face despite the vibrating and twitching to which our eyes are always prone, as well as the bad lighting or background movement which can often distort the view.

To experience your capacity for visual attention, look at an object in a room. Then change the viewing conditions. Have someone wave something in front of the object or turn the lights off and on rapidly.

Try viewing different objects while you move about. Any sport that includes playing with a ball requires a considerable amount of visual attention. You must focus clearly on the ball while you ignore irrelevant objects and movement in the visual field. As you play, you are exercising the brain circuits that control visual attention. The more you play, the higher you will raise the standards to which these neurons adapt.

Where in the brain are these circuits? Scientists have uncovered evidence that neurons in the top and back of the cortical mantle control our visual attention abilities.[1] If you put your hand on the back of your head and then slide it just up and over the top, it will lie over the part of the brain that controls visual attention.

We know this in part because artists who have recovered from a stroke on one side of this area of the brain lose and eventually regain their visual attention abilities. Right after the stroke, when this brain area is not functioning, the artists cannot attend to one half of the visual world. Any paintings they produce have no detail on the half controlled by the affected portion of the brain. As the function of the tissue slowly returns, the artists' visual attention improves, and they can again paint a full picture.

Feature Analysis

Another example of the brain's spatial abilities is *feature analysis*. Two neuroscientists who shared a Nobel prize—David Hubel and Torsten Wiesel—discovered that the brain areas just underneath the bone at the back of our heads divide up and define the features of our spatial worlds.

Some of these brain cells become activated when you look at a simple line, while others are active when you see a moving line. Moreover, the brain cells that are exercised by a vertical line are not the same as the ones exercised by a slanted or horizontal line. By having cells that respond to so many features of the visual world, your brains are able make sense of the definition of spaces in that world.

Look at this triangle: You just turned on at least 3 different sets of cells that helped your brain register the spaces defined by the 3 different lines. (Actually, you exercised other brain cells that respond to corners, too.) Now close your eyes and imagine the triangle you just saw. By having exercised your brain's "feature detectors" over a lifetime of contact with your spatial world, you have developed cell memories of these lines. These memories allow you to imagine the lines at will.

You can easily exercise these feature detectors and stimulate their memories. Focus on an object—say a chair—and think about its contours. These are the edges that define the object in space. Trace the object in space with your finger—slowly. Be sure to capture all the features that define its shape.

Now close your eyes and imagine that object in space. Picture it smaller than it is. Now larger. You are stimulating the memory capacity of your feature detectors. What is interesting about these smaller and larger images is that they do not take up proportionately smaller and larger amounts of circuitry in the brain. The different sizes merely exercise different cells. By shifting the memory of your perceptions in this way, you can thus stimulate a variety of brain cells. Furthermore, as I mentioned in the Preface, Harvard scientist Stephen Kosslyn has shown that imagining these visual images exercises your brain more than simply seeing them.

BENEFITS OF IMPROVED SPATIAL FUNCTIONS

Picture yourself as a movie camera operator filming an actor—also yourself—from a distance above. You can see your actor-self, a rather small figure on your mind's monitor screen, moving about in her own world. But there is no script. This is real life.

You see the actor, who is not familiar with this area of town, stop someone and ask for directions to a restaurant. The directions are rather lengthy, and they involve a lot of signposts along the way. You watch as the actor (you) starts along the path while scrutinizing the area for signs. Just up ahead and to the right—which you can see from your camera position, but which the actor cannot see—a police action blocks the route. You watch as the actor comes upon the road block, and then walks into a dead end trying to get around it. If only you could talk to your actor-self and show this person the entire plan that you can see, you could direct your actor-self through an easy detour.

From the camera position, you can see the entire plan in its spatial layout. The earthbound actor can see only what is immediately before her. If that route is blocked, the actor has no "mind's eye" vision as a guide.

This little vignette is really a metaphor for life in a spatial world. The camera operator is analogous to the "mind's eye" vision that all of us have—but to widely varying degrees of facility. Without access to a facile mind's eye, some problems are more difficult to solve because not only do you keep running into dead ends, but you have trouble imagining ways to get out of them. If you could enhance the functioning of certain spatial abilities, you would find that some problems are not really so difficult after all.

In a real world, "mind's eye" spatial problems include: The designing of a business hub, a personnel shift-work strategy, sketching an idea in order to communicate it to an associate, a data presentation, or being able to envision the "big picture" instead of getting lost in the details when you listen to directions to a restaurant. "Mind's eye" problems range from the simple—as in rotating a machine part in your mind to see how to position it in a tight space—to the complex, in which you might imagine an advertising idea before you even try to translate it to the sketch board. Spatial functions involve so much of our lives, it is difficult to think of a problem that does not include them.

GAMES AND EXERCISES TO DEVELOP SPATIAL BRAIN FUNCTIONS

Level One

Feature Calisthenics

You can do these exercises at your desk whenever you want to take a short break.[2] Sit in a comfortable position. To focus your mind, take three deep breaths and exhale each through your nostrils. Close your eyes. Imagine in your mind's eye a triangle defined by three equal black lines. Make the triangle large. Make the triangle small. Now make the triangle of a size that will make it possible for you to see it plus three other equal-size shapes in your mind's eye, once you have arranged them in a row. Place the triangle on the left, put a square the same size next to it, next to the square put a circle, and next to the circle put an oval. Keep all of them in your mind's eye vision. Now fill the square with black. Fill the oval with white. Make the triangle suddenly get large and swallow the other shapes.

Try your own variations. One that is a little more challenging is to imagine an object—say a book. Now turn the image into its corresponding two-dimensional shape—a vertical rectangle. Now imagine the rectangle growing in the third dimension until it becomes the book once again. Try this exercise with your car (circles and other more complex contours), with your house (triangles and four-sided figures), and with your bathtub (whatever shape that is).

Doodling

If you aren't running the meeting, and you don't have a significant part in it, you can exercise your brain's spatial abilities by doodling. This way, instead of processing only verbal or logical information during the meeting, you can provide your brain with extra spatial stimulation. At one meeting, try connecting geometric shapes into interesting combinations. At another, draw irregular contour lines to make interesting forms. At yet another, attempt to sketch the meeting table or the profile of the person in front of you. And remember to be discreet.

Mental Furniture Arrangement

Take a short break to do this one. Picture your living room or office (or any familiar room with furniture and wall hangings). Clearly imagine every piece of furniture in that room. One way to help yourself do this is to imagine yourself in that room looking at each piece of furniture. Another way is to imagine that you are filming the room and all its furniture from above. If you find any of this hard to do, then go into the actual room and look around to get a clear visual image of each piece. Your visual memory should now be fresh enough to enable you to do this exercise successfully.

While you have this room in your mind's eye, remove a piece

of furniture and visualize the empty spot. Now remove another piece of furniture. Then another. Gradually strip the room of furniture. Remove any floor covering or wall hanging and picture the room in your mind as it would appear bare.

Now put all the furniture and all the wall hangings back, but in different places. Picture a completely rearranged room. You may surprise yourself and decide you like the mental arrangement enough to make it a reality. But that of course is only a side benefit; the important thing is to exercise the spatial abilities that allow your mind to envision new configurations.

Finally, picture the rearranged furniture being returned to their original positions. Don't worry about making mistakes at first. As you improve, you'll notice that the images appear more quickly, and you'll find it easier and easier to reproduce reality in your mind's eye. Your spatial abilities are quite strong if, for a complicated room, you can visualize everything in its correct place.

Level Two

Profiles of Space

Betty Edwards[3] has a wonderful technique for getting people to shut out verbal thoughts in order to exercise spatial thoughts—doubly wonderful in that it doesn't take much time, or equipment. All you need is a flat surface, paper, pencil, and enough time to take a short break from your daily routine.

Edwards asks that you draw a face-vase. She suggests that you start on the left side of the paper if you are right-handed and the right side if left-handed. You begin by drawing a profile.

You should draw a profile of the oddest face you can imagine —a witch, a zombie, a monster. Since this is not the crucial spatial part of the exercise, you can use your verbal (nonspatial) abilities to name the parts of the face as you go down the profile: forehead, eye inset, nose, lips, chin. You should also add whatever embellishments you think are fun: double moles, protruding lips, wrinkles. Make the face complex, but be sure you still recognize it as a face. An example is shown on the following page:

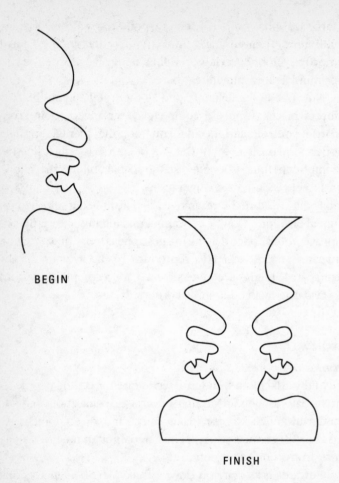

BEGIN

FINISH

After you finish this profile of a weird face, add horizontal lines at top and bottom for the vase. Now you are ready to copy the profile in reverse. This is when you shift into spatial mode. You are simply trying to move the line in direct opposition to the contours on the profile. As you do this, you must avoid thinking of eyes or noses or lips, and think only of shapes. You are using spatial thoughts and exercising those neural circuits that deal with spatial relations: visual attention, feature detectors.

Feel the verbal thoughts disappear as you make your copy. You might find a pleasurable sensation occurring as analytic tensions relax in favor of pure spatial relations. The sensation of exercising pure spatial functions can be quite rewarding, especially if you are used to a verbal mode of analysis.

Improvement on this brain exercise is easy to monitor. One way is to clock how much time it takes to complete the copy side of the profile. The degree of accuracy in the copy is also a key feature of your measure of improvement. It may take a while to get the exact opposite contour down the first time you do this brain exercise. As you improve, however, your movements become more automatic. As this happens, the neurons that control your spatial abilities are adapting to the spatial stimulation and developing memories of your improvement.

Sprouts

Martin Gardner, the puzzle maven for *Scientific American*, tells us (in his wonderful book, *Mathematical Carnival*, NY: Knopf, 1975) that the game of sprouts was invented Tuesday afternoon, February 21, 1967, at Cambridge University when a mathematics professor and a graduate student had finished their tea in the department lounge. They were doodling to see if they could figure out a new paper-and-pencil game. They came up with "sprouts," and the game just took off at Cambridge. After Gardner wrote about it, thousands more began to enjoy this simple spatial game.

The game is composed of dots and lines (straight or curvy) and can be made simple or complex depending on how many dots you begin with—three or four are recommended. Each player takes turns making a "move," which consists of drawing a line that joins one dot to another dot or to itself (by drawing a loop which closes back on itself). After you draw your line, you place a new dot anywhere along the line. In making a move, you have two restrictions: (1) A line cannot cross itself, cross a previously drawn line, or pass through a previously made dot; and (2) No dot may have more than three lines growing out of it. With these rules, there will be fewer and fewer ways to draw a sprout as the game progresses, though the number of "moves" varies with the way each sprout is drawn. Eventually, only one move remains. Depending on how you want to play, either the winner or the loser is the last person to make this move; thus, you can change the strategy of play. A little competition like this gets the adrenaline flowing and speeds the development of memory formation in neurons that handle spatial information. An example of a sprouts game is shown below:

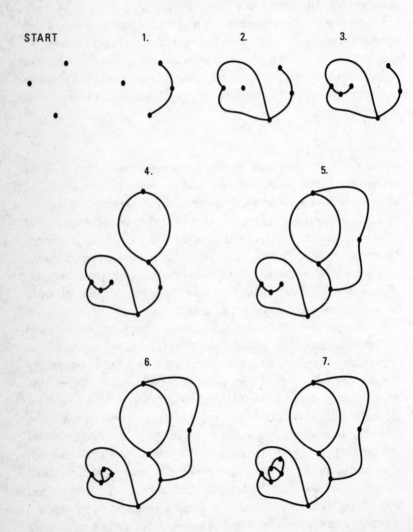

An example of a sprouts game. Each numbered drawing represents a separate "move."

Jigsaw Puzzles

Brain exercise can be quite simple—mere extensions of childhood games. This one is similar to portions of the IQ test that examine spatial abilities. It is fun and restful, and it's good to have on hand for a quick break from your work activity.

For this exercise in contours (edges of shapes), it is best that you use a rather simple jigsaw puzzle with few pieces. If you take great delight in jigsaw puzzles and love the ones with a thousand or more pieces, you can work up to them at your leisure. But for now, you will want something that can be pulled out of a desk drawer for a short brain stimulation break.

This kind of brain exercise is best done in a systematic way. To get started, you should first finish the puzzle, or, if you do not have the time to do this, extract all the edge pieces and put them together to form a frame. Now remove either the top or bottom row of edge pieces, break them apart, and turn them over so you do not see any of the printed design.

As an exercise in pure contours, simply fit the row of overturned pieces together while you time yourself. Keep a record of your time. Now take the pieces apart again and see if your assembly time improves. Then do the same thing with the other row. See if your first time for this other row is better than your first time for the original row.

This exercise has any number of variations. After you put together a row of overturned pieces, take them apart, mix them up, turn them right side (picture side) up, and try again. You will find out if the picture patterns enhance or interfere with your appreciation of shapes by the corresponding changes in your recorded times. If your times are better, you can bet that the brain functions that give us pattern recognition abilities are helping the functions that deal with pure contours. If not, you can always go back to exercising the pure contour recognition function.

If you keep a record of your times over a period of weeks or months, this exercise can also be a good test both of overall improvement and of the occasional episode of brain fatigue. Even if your improvement is generally consistent, there will always be fluctuations corresponding to the degree of mental alertness you have on any given day. Unusually good or bad scores don't indicate drastic improvement or decline—just mental quickness or its opposite, mental sludge, probably for reasons having to do with how rested, relaxed, and "up" you are on that particular day.

Level Three

Spatial Mapping: Do It While You Shop

The beauty of this exercise is that you can do it while you are shopping for groceries. It requires only a little more time than you would normally spend. If that gives you pause, think how much less overall time you are spending by working on two activities at once —shopping and brain exercise. Besides, what else can you do to make grocery shopping more fun that also rewards your brain?

The strategy most people use when they go shopping is to travel up and down the aisles until they find all the food they want. This is called the algorithm method, after the computer term for a systematic strategy.

Another strategy is to use a checklist (e.g., a shopping list). Items are checked off as they are dropped into the cart. The checklist method is usually automatically combined with the aisle method to reduce the amount of work your brain has to do.

Brains tend to take the easy way out if you don't stimulate them. They don't want to exercise their memory if they don't have to. As dreary as shopping is, I personally understand why brains behave this way. At the very least, it conserves energy by giving nerve cells little extra work to do.

The method in my madness is to ask the little-worked neurons to do something useful while you shop—that is, to remember where things are located in space. This will stimulate your spatial memory.

It is best to start with six to eight grocery items until you get the hang of it. (Also, do this at a time when your supermarket is not so crowded.) You can work with those groceries you usually buy each week or the ones that you only buy occasionally. (It is more difficult to work with the occasional items.) Bring your cart to the center of a supermarket where you have a good idea of the layout. The items should be located in different places in the store. If you are too efficient and include items which are all located in one place, you will not stimulate your brain as much.

Go retrieve one of the items and return your cart to the center of the store. Then retrieve another item. Try not to refer to your grocery list. If you have to look at the list, at least do not check off the item. Continue retrieving until you have finished with all six to eight items in your cart. You will not look silly because no one will know you are doing a brain exercise. They will all think you are shopping like they are. The difference is that your brain is improving.

The object of this exercise is to build up a mental map of the foods in the store. It obviously involves memory as well as spatial abilities and is thus useful for two kinds of mental stimulation. Other kinds of memory stimulation will be provided by exercises in chapter seven, the memory chapter.

Improvement on this exercise is easy to measure. Try it until performance is smooth and requires little time or hesitation. You don't have to high-tail it through the supermarket to prove anything. This is not a road race. The point is to achieve smooth performance. When you no longer hesitate on six to eight items, expand your list to increase your exercise. You may find that, as you improve, you no longer need to carry a list at all.

Spatial Mapping: Do It While You Drive

The purpose of this exercise is also to develop your mental mapping system, but in a slightly different way. This exercise is related to the previous one, but as the title suggests you do it in a car—on short or long trips. It could make a daily commute a little more interesting, and it will certainly help develop your spatial abilities so that you are better at getting "the big picture"—the aerial view discussed in the vignette about the camera.

The idea is to change a mental *route* into a mental *map*. As you travel from points A to B on a mental route, you think about the things you always see: billboards, buildings, streetsigns, and the like. You often use a route strategy to give directions to someone: Take a left at the black glass skyscraper, go two blocks, turn right on Howard Street and pass McDonald's, Wendy's, and Burger King until you get to the house with the giant pine tree in front.

To change from the route to the map, lift yourself in your mind's eye up and away from the route and see it as it might be seen from a camera on a blimp above. You will see the whole layout as on a map. To give your mental map a frame of reference, picture the compass directions printed on it.

Mentally draw the route from beginning to end on this map. Try to see the route as it changes direction. Think about the changing direction as you would a moving contour line. See it etching its way along, creating the route outline in your mind.

Once you have drawn your normal route on the mental map, draw another mental route on the same map. Use the same starting and ending positions, but draw (in your mind) a route you normally do not take. It does not matter whether this route would take you out of your way. The point is to build up your mental mapping system. Try it for a third route, and a fourth. It should get easier to do the more you stimulate these spatial abilities.

Test yourself when you get home or to your destination. Draw your mental map on paper in the same compass frame. Compare this transferred mental map to a real map of the area. As your brain's spatial functions improve, your mental maps will look more and more like the real maps. You may also find that your sense of direction has improved far beyond what you knew it to be.

By the way, if this exercise takes away any ability to be alert while you drive, consider doing it at home or in your office. Brain exercise should help the mind without harming the body.

Computer Games that Enhance the Brain's Spatial Abilities

Remember all the hype about the "paperless office" in which computers were to take over all bureaucratic functions and leave people free to do only the high-level thinking? Well, it hasn't happened, and most of us actually have more paper around in the form of printouts. Even more ironic is that one of the best devices readily available to stimulate our brains' spatial abilities sits around all day doing routine office accounting or word processing. It takes a big load off our hands, true, but then we never seem to take advantage of what it can do for our minds.

It is likely that you have a computer either in your office or at home. If it is in your office, it is usually always running or awaiting your next entry. That is a wonderful state of affairs! If you load a computer game onto it, before everyone else gets settled in in the morning, or any other time when the machine is not in use and you could use some mental stimulation, you're in for ten or twenty minutes of exercise that will wake up that lethargic brain.

A list of video or computer games that exercise your brain's spatial functions would itself take up several volumes. But a few examples will suffice to illustrate the kinds of stimulation that speed the flow of blood to areas of the brain that are critical for daily life in a spatial world.

The first example is computer based, but comes packaged separately as a real game. It is the Simon game, a battery-powered disk divided up into four different-colored pie wedges. You place it on your lap or on a table and start it, and it flashes a light in one of the wedges. You then copy the sequence of lights by pressing the wedge that has just lit up. If you get it right, it then flashes two wedges— the first one and another one chosen at random. If you get both of those right, it then flashes three wedges, and so forth.

Since the wedges are chosen at random, the spatial positions you have to copy rapidly become more complex as the number of wedges increase. This is a hard game to excel at if you think about it analytically. To do well, you must shift into spatial mode, much like you did when you copied the profile on the face-vase. Improvement in your brain's spatial abilities is built right into the game. The better you become, the more lighted wedges you must copy.

Then there is the computer game of Caverns. Many variations exist, but they usually require you to follow various clues that will lead you into an imaginary cave where treasure is hidden—and various dangers lurk. Once inside the (mental) cave, it is important that you build a mental map quickly to avoid getting chased by gnomes with knives or hatchets. You also need to find your way out again with the treasure.

One interesting variation on this game is when the cave is never shown to you: You build it completely in your mind. The best part about it as brain exercise is that it hardly feels like exercise. It is fun. The excitement of finding the hidden treasure and avoiding danger forces you to build a mental map of the cave without your even thinking about it. Improvement is easy to see when you find and extract the treasure with less and less difficulty. You can often set your own game "level" to let the computer know how advanced you are. This is another way of showing yourself just how far your brain has developed. A variant is the Wizardry game, in which you have to find your way through forests and deserts.

A related game is Mazes, but its kinship lies not so much in the game as in the brain exercise. On the screen, you are shown a 3-D view of what you would see if you were in a real maze. For example, looking north in a maze, you might come across a corridor that goes both east and west. If you turn to the right (east), you might see the eastern corridor trailing off with a single left turn (north). If you face back in the opposite direction (west), you would see the left turn into that north-south corridor from which you just came.

Because it is about space, this game is a lot harder to describe in words, which are controlled by a different part of your brain. Once you get into it, the stimulation of spatial abilities is pure. The better you become at building mental maps, the easier it will be to play. If you are looking for the added stimulation of competition, a variant is Maze Wars, a maze game in which two or three can play.

One of my recent favorites is Tetris, in which you have to orient a series of shapes into filled rows before they fall out of position. The game is over when the shapes stack up and reach the top of the screen. If you fill the rows first, however, they disappear, leaving you more room (and more time) to get more points. With time, the shapes fall faster and faster, forcing you to exercise your spatial planning abilities.

Computer games have so many brain stimulation advantages, I could not be more enthusiastic about them. For one, they are easy to set up, especially if your computer is already up and running. Often, the only thing required is to pop in a disk. If you have a very strict time budget to observe, you might have enough room on your financial planning disk, say, to copy a computer game onto it. Then, whenever you get stuck or tired, you can bring up the game for a few minutes of relaxation. This can recharge your batteries enough to get you back to your financial planning with gusto.

For spatial stimulation at home, Nintendo games are excellent. They create a delightful visual/aural environment while they stimulate spatial motor coordination. And don't be surprised if you are a lot slower (and score fewer points) than your kids, who operate more in a spatial mode than analytical and verbal adults. In fact, you might consider the smoothness (and point scoring ability) of your kids to be the spatial ideal for which you need to strive. (And if you respectfully elicit their help right from the start, they will enjoy becoming the teacher and may not taunt you or jeer at your rank beginner's performance.)

Even the oldies like Pac-Man, or any of the shoot-em-up games, activate neurons that process spatial information as they force you to follow and manipulate images on the screen. The games are relaxing because they shift your brain out of analytical thought modes and into purely spatial modes.

The playing of these games is thus one of the best things to do for your brain during that afternoon "down time" when you do not want to sleep but do need something to take your mind off what you have been working on. It can put your brain into a relaxing "flow state" that can refresh you for the late afternoon push.

Another great advantage is the ease with which you can monitor your brain improvement. Computer games often have different skill levels, and some of them will keep a record of your score on previous plays, thus allowing you to track your improvement over time. Moreover, you can always find a computer game that suits you to a tee. They are fun, and improvement is quick when brain exercise is that rewarding. A computer may be a great device for financial planning or word processing, but you will find many more rewarding uses for it if you let it help you exercise your brain.

CHECK YOUR PROGRESS

If you perform the brain exercises described above, and you monitor your improvement at every level, you will have a good idea of your progress. Or you may find that daily life and the business world test your spatial abilities so often that testing isn't even necessary after a while. You will know, for example, whether you are able to grasp the trend charts faster or to sketch a layout of the branch network with more ease.

However, tests are a valuable tool for making you focus your efforts on those mental abilities you have been trying to improve. Some would even argue that the very act of *taking* the exam hones your abilities further. For those of you who think you would benefit from performing under test conditions, and are curious about how you would score on a formal, objective measurement of spatial abilities, the balance of the chapter consists of a series of such tests, many of which are adapted from books by Jim Fixx, Martin Gardner, Howard Gardner, and E. Emmett.[4] There are no standard scores and no reason for you to feel pressure to perform at a higher level. The point is only to show how various spatial abilities come together to help you solve different problems. Tests like these are helpful in that they can even make you more aware of the spatial functions you use in everyday life.

In the first section, a special tension between two modes of brain functions has been created. Your tendency to use one or the other will tell you a lot about how your mind normally operates. It is perfectly fine to operate in either mode. These few questions will merely give you insight into your natural approach. With this insight, you will more easily be able to switch in and out of the two modes as you seek to solve everyday problems.

TWO MODES OF THOUGHT

5.1. Howard Gardner suggests that in your mind's eye you should take a sheet of paper and fold it in half. Then fold it in half again twice. How many rectangles are marked by creases after this final fold?

5.2. Find the length of the diagonal indicated on the opposite page:

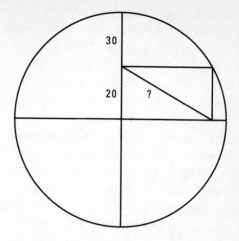

5.3.   Over the side of a ship in port hangs a rope ladder with rungs half a foot apart. The tide rises at the rate of 9 inches per hour. At the end of 4 hours how much of the rope ladder will remain above water, assuming that 20 rungs were above water when the tide began to rise?

Answers:

5.1.   8 rectangles.

5.2.   50 units. The rectangle's diagonal is also a radius, which in this example is equal to 20 units plus 30 units.

5.3.   While the ship is afloat, the water level in relation to the ship always stays the same. Anything affixed to the ship—like a rope ladder—is afloat with the ship. The 20 ladder rungs that were above water when the tide began to rise are still above water.

Explanation

These three problems are best solved by using your brain's spatial functions—by putting the scene in your mind's eye. The tension I was trying to create was between spatial and mathematical modes of thinking. You can tell which problem-solving mode of thinking your brain favors by seeing which way your mind automatically leaned. If you solved the problems quickly, you probably have a well-developed spatial mode of thinking. If this is the case, you might also be shying away from problems at the office that are solved with math/logic abilities, and you may need to spend more time with the math/logic chapter of this book.

If instead you tried to dredge up old math memories, and you shy away from visual or spatial presentations at work, you may want to spend more effort on the spatial exercises in this chapter. You should not be afraid of your weaknesses to the point where you overrely on your strengths. By becoming sensitive to how your mind solves problems—the kind of thinking it favors—you can tell which brain exercises you need to emphasize.

Think about how you solved the paper folding problem. You could do it in your mind's eye by mentally folding and unfolding the paper and visualizing the image of the resulting creases. Or you could have used math/logic abilities and multiplied $2 \times 2 \times 2$ as you fold each section in half. Some mathematicians begin to solve the circle puzzle by calculation. If you lean toward spatial thought, however, you could easily flip the diagonal of that rectangle so that it becomes obvious that it is also a radius and thus has the same length as the given radius. In fact, it is interesting that children who have not had extensive grounding or practice in math tend to see the solution right away. The classic boat problem is not solved with math calculations, though people who shy away from mental images tend to try. If you visualize the boat and everything on it (including the rope ladder) floating on the water—rising and falling with the water level—it is easier to see the solution.

Relax and find your tendencies. The more you identify your current levels and leanings, the better position you will be in to see what you need to do to improve.

MORE PROBES OF THE BRAIN'S SPATIAL FUNCTIONS

5.4. Imagine yourself standing in front of your house (or in front of a house you know well). Bring a clear image of the house into your mind. How many windows are in the front? The back?

5.5. Arrange ten coins to make a triangle like the one below.

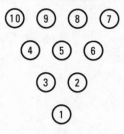

Now, by moving only 3 coins, turn the triangle upside down.

5.6. Draw 4 straight lines through all 9 spots without lifting your pen from the paper.

5.7. Without using a pen to mark the page, count the number of triangles contained in this figure.

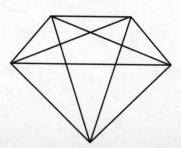

5.8. Make a square exactly twice the size of this one without including any of the circles in its area.

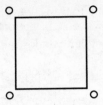

5.9. See into how many pieces you can divide a fresh cherry pie with 6 straight cuts of the knife. The pie is goopy, so you can't rearrange or pile pieces after a cut. The standard pie cut shown below gives you 12 pieces, but you can get a lot more.

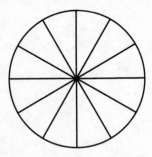

5.10. Here's a spatial reasoning question that first intrigued me when I was a teenager:

If a mirror reverses your image from right to left and vice versa (i.e., right hand looks like a left hand, et cetera), why doesn't it do the same thing from top to bottom?

Answers:

5.4. Only you know.

5.5. Move coins 1, 7, and 10 to the positions shown.

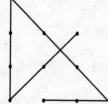

5.6.

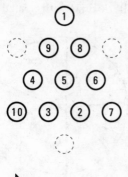

5.7. The figure has 35 triangles. If you are having trouble remembering the triangles once you spot them, try numbering the small areas and write down the combinations that make up each triangle you spot.

5.8. Add on triangular sections in the way shown below.

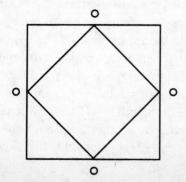

5.9. If you don't care about having even pieces, you can get as many as 22 with 6 straight cuts. The idea is to make sure each cut intersects every other cut, without any two intersections coinciding. It doesn't exactly make you gracious as a host, but then we are only dealing with spatial concepts and not real pies.

5.10. It will. You only have to take the plane of viewing into consideration. If you put a mirror on the floor and do a headstand on it, it will reverse your image from top to bottom.

Our brains control many different kinds of spatial knowledge. The problems you will be called upon to solve in business or personal life can involve pure spatial abilities, a combination of spatial and verbal abilities, or a mix of spatial and mathematical abilities. Problems in design, or the fitting together of patterns or parts, are purely spatial. Problems that involve description of a layout or image—for example, trying to convey your concept of an advertising strategy—entail both spatial and verbal abilities. Problems that use math or logic abilities sometimes benefit from a spatial approach. And advertising and marketing strategies are often better communicated by the graphic arts than with tables of numbers or statistics.

You can force your brain to exclude verbal and analytical thought while you shift to a spatial mode of doing things. This is wonderful exercise for your spatial abilities, but you should also keep your natural tendencies in mind. If you are relying on your spatial tendencies to the exclusion of other brain functions, perhaps it is time to exercise those other brain functions. This is what the rest of the book is all about.

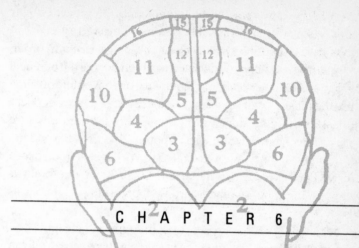

C H A P T E R 6

Talking to Your Brain

The brain function that truly sets us apart from animals is our
ability to use language. The apes who learned sign language
don't even come close to our abilities. Dolphins and whales,
who have large and complex brains and sophisticated patterns of
musical communication, simply do not possess the richness of communication inherent in our languages. It is for its uniqueness to the
human species that we place a premium on language ability—the
written word, the verbal reply. I like the way Bertrand Russell put
it: "No matter how eloquently a dog may bark, he cannot tell you
that his parents were poor but honest."

You feel the importance of language when you have to give a
lecture or presentation, write a report, or convince a colleague that
your idea will fly; when you read a memorable passage in a poem

or book; when you watch a child's excitement at the growing ability to modulate sounds into words that produce a desired effect.

Poets have a special sensitivity to the meanings, rhythms, order, and sounds of words.[1] They understand to a high degree the potential of language to excite our emotions, amuse us, or convey information. Poets are the musicians of language. Though most of us are not poets, we all possess these sensitivities to varying degrees, even if we are unaware of them, they have an effect upon us that goes beyond the surface meaning of the words we hear (or read). For example, speech is perceived by us in two ways: While one part of our brain is analyzing its meaning, another part is appreciating it simply as sounds.

By heightening your awareness of both sound and meaning, you can train your brain to become more facile with language. You can become more sensitive to language and thus better able to convince a colleague of your idea or describe your advertising strategy in words that capture the imagination of your audience.

LANGUAGE IN THE BRAIN

From the research on language disorders, we now have tantalizing clues about the brain's language functions and the best ways to exercise them. We know that in most people language circuits are on the left side of the brain. We also know more about how these circuits control the fine subfunctions of language.

LANGUAGE ORGANIZATION

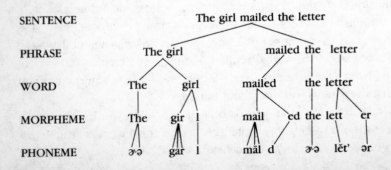

According to Noam Chomsky, a renowned linguist at the Massachusetts Institute of Technology, we are born with an innate ability to acquire language. Every time we hear someone utter something in our own language, our brains dissect and analyze the utterance. Even the basic sounds of language—the phonemes—have intelligible meaning to our brains far beyond that of all the nonlanguage sounds we can hear.

Our language circuits have their own memories and can continually absorb new words. If the new words are in our native language, we have no trouble putting together the phonemes (basic sounds) and morphemes (word units), since they are constructed from parts that are already in our language memories. The new words, however, stimulate connections at the higher levels of language. They enable us to construct greater numbers of phrases and sentences. As these higher level processes are stimulated, our brains can only become better.

The Left and the Right of It

Most any way you slice the brain, you will find paired structures. Your brain has two hemispheres, each with suborgans matched on the other side. The only unmatched structure is the pineal gland, and its singularity led philosophers to designate it as the seat of the soul. But with this (mostly) symmetrical architecture in the brain, it came as a great surprise when language functions were found only on one side.

If I could, I would bet that your language functions are located on the left side of your brain. The odds are certainly with me on this one: Over 95 percent of all right-handers and about 70 percent of lefties have speech and language controlled on the left side.

If you were about to have brain surgery, you would probably undergo the Wada test to see which side of your brain controls your ability to speak. You would lie on your back, extend both arms, and begin counting backward from one hundred by threes. Meanwhile, the surgeon would inject a drug in the artery that feeds the left half of your brain. The drug acts like a sleeping pill and would temporarily put that half to sleep.

Because your left brain controls your right arm, that arm would fall limp when that side of the brain went to sleep. If you could still do the counting chore, that would mean that your language functions are on the awake right side. But, more often than not, you will stop counting as your language functions fall asleep on the left side of your brain. It was this test, given to hundreds of patients, that confirmed the earlier clinical findings about where the language circuits are.

If you were at an important meeting in which you were presenting charts of your company's business and profit trends, you would be simultaneously using language and spatial functions to describe those graphics. Your left brain would be analyzing the verbal description and speaking about it while your right brain was relating to the contours and shapes on the graphs. All the while, the two halves of your brain would be "talking" to each other through millions of nerve fibers that cross from one side to the other.

The importance of this "crosstalk" was discovered in patients who had to undergo operations for epilepsy. In many of these operations, the crosstalk fibers were severed to prevent the spread of the epileptic storm. After the operation, the two halves of these patients' brains could still carry out their normal functions, but they could no longer "talk" to each other.

Many of these patients agreed to being tested by having different images presented to each brain hemisphere. For example, a kitchen scene might be shown to the right hemisphere while an art studio was shown to the left. When the patients were asked to point to a relevant picture that corresponded to the image, their right brains (kitchen scene) might direct their left hands to point to a toaster, while their left brains (art studio) would direct their right hands to point an easel. (Remember, right and left brain halves control opposite hands.) But, if they were asked to *say* what they saw, they would reply, "I saw the artist painting something, so I pointed to the easel. Artists have to go to the kitchen to get something to eat."

The mute right brain could not say what it saw, but it was good at recognizing graphics, and it did have an awareness of the images that got to it. The talkative left brain liked to flaunt its language control, but it also saw the spatial images.[2]

These findings tell us what happens when you exercise your language abilities. You strengthen the circuits on the side of your brain that controls various language functions, which is probably the left. In doing so, you improve your abilities to translate graphic charts into words, or to write those critical reports with ease.

Dividing Up the Left: Language Functions of the Brain

The left brain is not some unitary mass that has one job to do. Each side of the brain has a regular program to instruct the opposite half of the body to move and to monitor its sensations. When you make piano movements with your right hand's fingers, brain cells in your left hemisphere are activated. If you stub your left big toe, your right brain registers the pain.

No one yet knows why the left brain takes on extra language functions. Harold Goodglass, director of Psychology Research at Boston Veterans Administration Medical Center, has devoted over thirty years to finding out exactly what the left brain does in the way of language. He tests patients who have varying degrees of left-brain damage to see which of their language functions have gaping holes.[3]

His testing has confirmed that speech processes are controlled by Broca's area, located in the left frontal areas of the brain very near the circuits that control motor ability for the mouth. Every time you utter a word, whether to give a speech or to order dinner, brain cells in Broca's area flare up with activity. The more you talk and articulate words, the more these cells are activated, and the more they can develop cell memories that improve your speech abilities.

Every time you understand what you hear or read, you have excited the brain cells in Wernicke's area, located in the top hind areas of the left temporal lobe (inside the skull near the top portion of your left earlobe). As you continue to activate these cells, they begin to adapt to the increased stimulation. As a result, you increase your comprehension of words.

When you learn the meaning of a new word, you build cellular bridges to the memory of that word in the vocabulary retrieval circuits of your brain. Every time you retrieve a difficult word whose meaning you already know, these cellular bridges are strengthened. The more you build and use your vocabulary, the better these circuits become. As vocabulary circuits improve, you become more facile with words.

Whenever you answer a question or reply to an insult, your brain has transferred the meaning of what you comprehended to your speech circuits for the reply. The transfer takes place through conduction circuits. The more you carry on conversation or answer questions, the more you exercise these conduction circuits, and the better you get at making verbal connections to what you hear or read.

And these are only the major categories. Language abilities are composed of many more nuances controlled by the brain. Although scientists have not unraveled all the mysteries of these nuances, there is growing evidence that most language abilities improve as language circuits are exercised.

BENEFITS OF IMPROVED LANGUAGE FUNCTIONS

Language touches most aspects of our lives. It provides us with tools for thinking and reasoning, for communicating our thoughts to others, and for understanding the thoughts of others.

Whether you are a lawyer, business executive, writer, actor, advertiser, chief cook, or bottle washer, you will benefit from enhanced language ability. It could happen at the manager's meeting, where you convince the director that your ideas are better than those of a manager in another section. Or you might describe your paintings so compellingly that the editor of that important art magazine decides to do a profile on you. You could also realize one day that your written reports are snappier and more convincing, or that you are getting more out of what you are reading. Or you could just feel better when you write a close friend a meaningful letter instead of calling on the phone.

Let's take an example from the legal system: Enhanced language will rarely win a hopeless case, but you can bet that illogical or imprecise language will lose a winnable one. You can guess what a judge would do if presented with two arguments, one containing language ease and precision and the other language abuse. If you have ever been on a jury, you know which lawyer is more convincing: the one who shows fluency of expression, not the one who stumbles over words.

EXERCISE YOUR LANGUAGE ABILITIES

Early in life, language may be learned not by learning rules of grammar and word composition but by learning analogies.[4] In essence, we may not unconsciously grasp concepts like "noun," "verb," and "preposition," but instead reason by deciding that "this word sounds like that word." If our brains are built to reason about language through contacts with it, we only need to increase those contacts to enhance our language abilities.

Traditional Contacts with Language

Reading

One time-honored way to enhance language contact is to increase the time you devote to reading books, magazines, and newspapers. Virtually any reading material will do, but keep in mind that poetry and fiction often come out of attempts to achieve subtleties with language and may therefore have more to offer you. But it is more important to read what you enjoy. You don't have to read the classics to improve your language abilities. Try to read whatever gives you a flow state—that exhilarating feeling of pleasure that absorbs you so completely that you forget your surroundings.

If you have little time to increase your reading, why not listen to books on tape while you are commuting? Check with your library or bookstore for availability. Many of those books you always wanted to read exist on cassette tape, waiting for you to enjoy them while you are driving or jogging.

Conversation

Another time-honored method is to seize increasing opportunities for conversation—not chit chat, but real dialogue. When you go out to have a good time, make sure the evening starts with at least one opportunity for real conversation. Having dinner together after you see that foreign film is one way to enter into a good conversation. Start or join a discussion group to multiply your language skills.

A New Language

If you really want to go all the way, try learning a new language. This will stimulate the language circuits in your brain in a fresh way. You will be amazed at how it increases your facility with your native tongue. You will begin to see hidden meanings and subtleties you would never have dreamed of before. Even the sounds of words take on a new life. If this were not enough, it can be exhilarating—a real flow state—to understand and be understood by native speakers of other languages. Travel becomes a lot more fun when you understand more of the cultural subtleties through the native language. International business becomes a lot easier when you can figure out what your foreign partners, buyers, or clients are saying in their native tongues. Anything you can do to give yourself a competitive edge is useful. And no surer way exists to build your brain's language circuits.

Getting started can be easy. Check with your local college or university. They often have adult language classes. Some city libraries have language tapes and records you can borrow. Check in the yellow pages for the language schools and instructional programs operating in your area. Or try your bookstores and book catalogs. You can also buy a number of private tutoring methods. Included among these are Berlitz Self Teacher, Living Language Series, Passport Books Listen and Learn series, Cortina, Hugo, and Barron's. Barron's, by the way, has twelve tapes per language and is often used to train diplomats.

Whatever method you choose, try to find a native speaker with whom you can converse. At the very least, get a friend to take the plunge with you. You will learn more at a much faster pace if you are pressed to use and think in the language you are learning.

If you do not have time to take courses, you can always listen to language tapes during your daily commute. Even this effort provides considerable stimulation of your brain's language circuits.

Word Games

Your daily paper will help you out here. Mine, for example, includes two crossword puzzles (syndicated by the *Chicago Tribune* and *Los Angeles Times*) and an anagram game (the object is to form several words by reordering the letters of a key word). For those of you who enjoy a little competition, the game of Scrabble can be included on this list.

Every once in a while you will run into a crossword snob. This is a person who will claim to complete a *New York Times* crossword in indelible ink on his ten-minute commute in the morning. Maybe he has gotten close to this level of performance once in seven years, and you can bet he will not let you watch him. So do not let crossword snobs inhibit you. I have always had a love of words and language but until recently a big fear of crosswords. When I think about this former fear, I believe it derived from my not being able to match the ability of my image of "real" crossword players. Even the late great Jim Fixx, noted author and Mensa member, complained of a "blind spot" with crosswords.

The fact is, crosswords are great tools for improving nuances of language. They exercise the brain cells involved in word retrieval, vocabulary, comprehension, and conduction. Each time you get a word that was a little difficult at the start, you feel a twinge of pleasure as the word retrieval brain cells become active.

Of course, the more you do it, the more you find little ways to gain word retrieval advantages. You begin to recognize themes that allow you to supply words you never would have gotten from the hints alone. You also become more sensitive to letter combinations and the probabilities that a certain letter will precede or follow another. (For example, an H is usually preceded by W, T, S, C, or P.) This sensitivity heightens your ability to retrieve words.

Relax and take it slowly. Crossword makers have a style of using and hinting at words that takes time to get used to. Understand that you will improve over time and that your first attempts at anything are bound to be less than you are capable of. To begin, allot yourself about a half hour so you do not drive yourself crazy with something that is supposed to be fun. You probably will not finish the puzzle, but you should view your performance as you do any measure of your brain's output. Whatever level of competence you have achieved is your base score, from which future improvements will be measured as you continue to exercise your language circuits.

Crosswords also provide another way to monitor your brain fatigue. Now that I have finally caught the spirit with the daily crosswords, I can just about predict how well I will do on any given day. On Fridays, when my language circuits are tired from a week of writing, I sometimes get stuck in the middle. On Mondays, when my language circuits have been refreshed from the weekend, I usually enjoy a high level of performance. In fact, it was on a Monday that I had my best performance: I did both crosswords in about forty minutes and only left out one letter in one of the puzzles.

Non-traditional Language Exercises

Articulation Aerobics

In addition to your mouth and jaw muscles, your neurons in Broca's area will get a real workout from this one. Brain cells in Broca's area control the articulation of speech. Every time you utter a word, you activate these cells. The trick is to increase the activity of these cells by providing a challenge to the way you speak.

Tongue twisters are words or sets of words that are difficult to articulate rapidly because of their strings of similar sounds. Tongue twisters are to speech what obstacle courses are to running. They both increase the challenge and, in doing so, improve the relevant circuits.

The point is to develop by the practice that comes with repetition. Keep trying each tongue twister until you can do it fluently. Be encouraged by small successes. You can only get better as you keep up the repetitions. Remember, any improvement in articulation ability means that the nerve cells controlling speech have developed their cell memories, enabling you to speak better when the occasion arises.

Also keep in mind that any exercise—especially brain exercise—entails a buildup of fatigue. This is natural, so do not be discouraged if you have trouble with an easy tongue twister after fifteen minutes of difficult ones. Not only will your tongue be tired, but the brain cells that control speech articulation will also be fatigued.

Twisting Your Tongue (and Brain)
Say each of the following aloud five times in rapid succession:

> Rubber baby buggy bumpers.
> Theo's theoretical theme songs.
> Shall she sell seashells?
> Shrewd Simon Short sewed shoes.

(Gyles Brandreth, in *More Joy of Lex*, informs us that the actual twister from which this last one is derived takes up about two pages of fine typescript and provides serious amusement if you are into marathon articulation aerobics.)

More tongue twisters:[5]

> The sixth sick sheik's sixth sheep's sick.
> The black blood of the bad black-backed bumblebee.
> This sixth thistle seems thick like the fifth thistle.
> Fresh fried fish don't flip like fresh fish flip.
> Sam shaves a cedar shingle thin.
> Sharon short-sheeted short Simon's short bed.
> Which is the witch that wished the wicked wish?

Try to say the following name five times as fast as you can: Peggy Babcock.

ONE of Alvin Schwartz's tongue twister games is useful not only for articulation exercise but for a general facility with words. At least two people need to play. One player makes up a twister. Then each other player, in turn, repeats the twister five times, as fast as possible. The first player to stumble loses and must drop out on that round. Schwartz suggests that the best way to make up a tongue twister is to write down a (sometimes senseless) string of words all beginning with the same letter or a similar sound. You will develop a twister in no time.

Listening to Your Voice

Before information about language reaches the brain's language centers for analysis, it must travel through the auditory system. Nerve fibers from sound receptors in the ears code the information and transfer it to areas of the brain that receive and analyze sound patterns. Auditory information is also channeled to the language centers, where it is decoded for the language content, if it has any.

This means that the fitness of the brain's auditory circuits affects its general language-processing abilities. The classic example is the deaf child who has difficulty learning to speak. Nothing is wrong with the brain per se, but the language centers have an easier time if they can "hear" the results of what the person is saying.

This is the concept of "feedback." As you produce language when you are learning to speak, you hear the sounds that you utter. If the sounds do not match those sounds that get what you want from your listeners, you can modify the sounds to make them correct.

The variety of feedback that you hear when you speak is composed of two kinds of sounds: One is what you hear through air conduction, and the other is what you hear through bone conduction. Actually, you hear both kinds through the same auditory system, but they reach the system in different ways.

You can separate the sources of sounds that you hear from your own voice. The way to hear your voice from air conduction alone —the way everyone else hears you—is to speak into a tape recorder and play it back. Your voice sounds "funny" to you this way because you rarely hear yourself without your own bone conduction.

To hear your voice primarily through bone conduction, simply plug your ears. Try it right now and read this passage aloud. Your voice will sound different to you because of your inability to hear the sounds carried through air waves, but it probably will not sound as "funny" as the tape recording.

You can become a better speaker and have more confidence in

your voice if you increase your brain's ability to distinguish the sounds that you utter. Try this quick and simple exercise:

Get a tape recorder and select a passage to read. The one you are reading right now will do just fine—or you may use the tongue twisters. Turn on the tape recorder and read the passage aloud. Then plug your ears and read the same passage aloud. When you play back the tape, you will probably hear subtle differences in your voice that you have never heard before. These differences arise from the different feedback your brain is receiving.

If you ever have to give a speech or say just a few words, try this recording technique beforehand—several times. As your brain becomes more sensitive to the qualities in your voice, your public utterances will become more dynamic. You might even notice a difference in your everyday conversations.

Vocabulympics

This exercise can be done in your head while you are driving to work, but you can also do it during a short break at your desk. By getting you to rearrange strings of letters and rapidly recognize words that are stimulated by the new strings, it strengthens your word retrieval abilities.

This is essentially a game of anagrams. Pick a word—any word. This is your "target word." For each of its letters (counting multiples only once), find two words beginning with that letter that are contained within the target word. The words should be at least three letters long, and you should not cheat by using simple plurals of words you have already used. As you get better, start listing three words for each letter, with words at least four letters long, and so on. Here's an example of the three word version:

REARRANGES

A	E	G	N	R	S
anger	earn	gear	near	rear	sang
area	eager	green	nags	rare	sear
arena	ease	garner	nares	range	seen

Remember not to overdo your exercises. Brain fatigue is similar to muscle fatigue. If you have not done any stretching since elementary school, you wouldn't dare try a split in your first workout. So don't strain your brain, trying to do the mental equivalent of a split—whatever that would be for you. If you can only pull up one three-letter word for each of the letters in your target word, let it go at that and consider that level to be your baseline. (Also consider that there might not *be* another word for that letter.)

Along these lines, if you feel like using a dictionary, it's certainly not a crime (unless you are driving). This is an exercise, not a test. If using a dictionary gets you a few extra words, then you are simply that many words smarter. You have built those cellular bridges to your brain's storage of words. In fact, the use of a dictionary might be considered part of your baseline. As your brain improves, and your word storage and retrieval circuits grow stronger, you will find yourself using reference tools less and less. Improvement *will* come with practice. You just have to trust your brain to develop with exercise.

Listening to Language

Have you ever wondered why some people never seem to understand what you say even though you've tried to say it in many different ways? Or why some people repeat what they've said to you even though you've indicated that you understood? Or why people sometimes seem to mean something other than what they say?

These problems happen to all of us at some time. One reason is that our brains operate on two levels: One produces the words we use to communicate, while the other provides the meanings. When the language output of the brain is analyzed, it has a *surface structure*, which is the collection and manner of words we use, and a corresponding *deep structure*, which is made up of the underlying meanings.

We tend to focus on the meaning (deep structure) of what someone says, while we pay only casual attention to its surface.[6] For example, say that you're not wearing a watch, but that you have just looked at a clock. If I then stop you on the street and ask "Are you wearing a watch?" you might well respond, "Yes, it's about four o'clock."

At this point our conversation is complete. We are both satisfied, despite the fact that you didn't answer my literal question. Your answer focused on what you perceived to be the deeper meaning in my question—namely, that I wanted to know what the time was, not whether you were wearing a watch. If you had instead focused on the surface of my question and answered: "No, I'm not wearing a watch," I would probably have felt misunderstood or frustrated, or thought that you were a little off.

Here's another example, taken from my dinnertable discussion with a friend who's a clinical scientist and noted author. We were talking about books, and I casually asked her, "Do you mind if I ask who your editor is?" She replied, "Yes. Her name is Jane Doe." (She gave the editor's real name.) If she had replied: "No, I don't mind," I would have had to ask another question to find out the name, which would have been annoying. By responding to the deep structure, she took care of a lot more business. Of course, if she *had* minded, she would have responded to my actual question with: "Yes, I mind." Whether someone responds to your surface or deep structure depends on how they feel about what you are asking.

You can get a lot more information about people if you sensitize yourself to the structure of their language. Suppose, as linguist Donald Spence does, a friend says to you: "I can't stomach any more fights with my husband." This probably means "I am tired of fighting," but it might have further meaning as well. If you notice that this friend often expresses her dismay about personal conflicts in terms of her "stomach" or "gut reactions," you may be able to read between the lines one day when she complains of nausea. In fact, you may understand something about her that even she herself does not. Such sensitivity to both the surface and the deeper meanings of language can make you very insightful in your dealings with people.

Therapists realize that form (surface structure) can be every bit as important as deep structure in providing insights about people. The best therapists, who are often accused of reading minds, are really only monitoring words closely. You can do this, too. For example, the subordinate who expresses a newfound delight in traveling for the company may be telling you she would like to be away from you for long stretches of time.

You cannot always be right about hidden meanings. After all, you cannot really read someone's mind. But by increasing your sensitivity to language, you can make your brain more aware of the underlying meanings of words used in social settings.

One of the best ways of increasing your sensitivity is simply to start thinking about surface and deep structure whenever you hear a conversation. It is probably not a good idea to start with conversations you yourself are having. The extra load of analysis could really throw you off balance. Instead, get your initial practice on conversations you overhear. You can also analyze your own conversations if you do so after the fact. Keep a journal and write down the hidden meanings in parentheses next to the literal conversation. You may be surprised at how quickly your brain increases its ability to dissect the true meanings of what people say to you.

Ambiguous Meanings

This is another simple exercise to get you started thinking about meanings. Name the meanings in these ambiguous sentences:

> Flying planes can be dangerous.
> The shooting of the hunters is terrible.
> The learning of the brain is easy.
> He chased after the postman running in his shorts.

You should always try to avoid ambiguous sentences in any type of writing that you do. Ambiguity is the opposite of accuracy. However, for the purpose of exercising your brain's language abilities, compose a few of these ambiguous sentences yourself. Make sure they have at least two meanings. You will rapidly become more sensitive to the meanings of your writings and utterances—and able to express yourself with greater precision once you've made a point of doing the opposite.

Insidious Language

In the natural cut and thrust of everyday life, you are sometimes subjected to insults that are buried in the language structure.[7] Something that sounds on the surface like a nice thing to say can really be a subtle insult.

For example, at work you might hear: "Don't you *care* about this company?"

The surface part of his statement asks whether you care about the company. Underneath it all, the attacker is implying:

You don't care about this company and I do.

You should care about this company; it's wrong of you not to.

Therefore, you should feel rotten.

Even more insidious: *Everyone understands why you are having such a hard time adjusting to this job.*

On the surface, it appears that the attacker is actually a caring person and is concerned with your adjustment in the new environment. But the deep structure says otherwise:

You are having a hard time adjusting to the job.

Everyone knows about the problem you have that's causing your difficulty in adjustment, so there's no point in trying to hide or deny it.

If your brain is not sensitized to the meanings in language, you *will* have a hard time adjusting to the job, especially if you take the bait. The worst thing to do in these situations is to protest loudly: "But I really do care . . ." or, "Really? Everyone knows about my difficulties?"

By becoming sensitive to hidden meanings, you can avoid taking the surface bait. As Suzette Haden Elgin, expert on verbal self-defense, suggests, you could reply: "It's a source of endless amusement to me how people in your situation might think I don't care about this company. . . ." Or, simply: "Thank you so much. I deeply appreciate your concern."

Every person has a skeleton or two in the closet. No aggressor in his right mind would question what the "situation" is that led him into his blunder. And the second reply simply steals the thunder from the aggressor's deep structure.

To sensitize your brain to these meanings, think through the surface and deep structures of the conversations you overhear. Write down anything particularly instructive from these or your own conversations. As your private conversation diary expands, you will find that your sensitivity to language has increased many times over. You may also find that your ability to work with your colleagues has improved, especially when they see that conventional language aggression does not work on you. You will elicit more respect, and it is all because your brain has been sensitized to the meanings in language.

CHECK YOUR PROGRESS

In school you are tested all the time, and in life too—in ways that are not so structured or formal, but may well be more meaningful. So keep in mind that the following tests are not any kind of absolute indicators of your language skills. Your language abilities will show themselves to you in what you are getting out of what you read, in how you handle the subtleties of language in conversation, in the degree of accuracy and fluency in your written reports, and in your ability to speak. But these tests may be interesting to you as measures of your improvement over time.

WEEKLY TESTS OF YOUR BRAIN'S LANGUAGE FUNCTIONS

1. After two weeks of attempts to complete your newspaper's daily crossword within twenty to thirty minutes (giving your brain cells time to rest over the weekend), try a crossword on a Monday or Tuesday morning as a test of your improvement. Calculate your score as the number of squares you leave unfinished, and determine whether you have improved over the two week practice period. Be sure to keep a record of your progress.

2. After one week of practice with the anagram game, give your brain a weekend off and then try your newspaper's anagram game Monday or Tuesday morning. If the game provides a time limit and an average number of words that can be made from the key word, use these to compare your scores. But do not be discouraged if you do not achieve the word count. Once again, the point is to measure your improvement—not the

absolute score. If you use the anagram game in this chapter, simply time yourself to see how fast you can find all the words.

3. You can play Scrabble against yourself if you keep two "hands" running for the entire game. This way, you at least know you have a consistent partner. Consistency has its advantages, the main one being that you can easily monitor your improvement from a steady baseline. The game itself helps you monitor your brain's word retrieval and memory abilities by giving you a method to score your word power. Higher scores will be achieved when you improve your brain's language circuits by making them respond to the extra demands.

You can, if you prefer, achieve the same goals by playing against other people. What you lose in consistency, you gain in the sharpening that comes with competition. The old cliché about competition "getting your juices flowing" has modern scientific backing. The rush of adrenaline that occurs on stressful occasions (such as competition) regulates the formation and storage of memories. Your word storage and retrieval abilities are enhanced as the excitement of playing a high-scoring word stimulates your adrenaline flow.

DEEP STRUCTURE TESTS

To see how well you understand the deep structures of language, try responding to these subtle language insults:[8]

A. "If you really cared about getting a raise, you'd make more phone contacts, like everyone else in the sales force does."

B. "A person who has mental discipline problems cannot possibly be expected to deal with the complexity in this particular department."

C. "Some supervisors would really get upset if their employees insisted on staying home so long after they have children."

D. "Don't you even care about the fact that enrollment has been dropping off in your classes?"

GOOD RESPONSES

A. *"Don't you feel that motivation can be shown in different ways? After all, it's the quality, not the quantity, of the contacts that leads to better sales, and if you'll examine my sales receipts, you'll see I'm doing as well or better than my colleagues."*

If this is in fact true, you have led your attacker down the path of your real value to the company. If it's not true, you had better make it clear that you plan to increase the quality or quantity of your contacts: "That seems a perfectly reasonable plan."

B. *"I couldn't agree with you more."*

You have created the impression that you share your attacker's concern for some other person who has serious mental discipline problems. This makes it difficult for your attacker, who should not be so foolish as to ask who you have in mind. And, to abuse you further, your attacker has to raise the stakes—quite difficult if you both agree on the matter.

C. *"Oh? It would be interesting to hear your opinion on the matter."*

You have caught your attacker off guard, and he will probably abandon all pretense to being the superior person to whom you should feel grateful.

D. *"That issue is certainly worth exploring. But before we can do so, there is the problem of actually finding the cause for this drop in enrollment you've noticed."*

You have taken all emotion out of the situation and forced your superior to focus on a real problem that you both can solve together.

WORD RECOGNITION AND RETRIEVAL TESTS

Here are a few questions that are good for testing, exercise, or just plain fun:[9]

6.1. How many words can you find from the English language that break the rule: I before E, except after C, or when sounded as "a," as in neighbor and weigh. Here are a few:

atheist	fancier	reinvent
caffeine	leisure	seize
either	protein	weird

6.2. The i-e rule and its exceptions may by itself give us headaches, but unfortunately the English language has many more inconsistencies that can lead to poor spelling. Solomon Lowe's *Spelling Book*, first published in 1755, tells us that eighteenth-century English was no less problematic. Lowe cites words with superfluous letters, and words that have the same sound but different spellings, as causes of many spelling problems. Here are some of the words he includes: duchess (spelled duchefs), achieve, carat and carot (the vegetable only had one r then), and coarse and course (spelled coarfe/courfe back then). The following words still give many of us trouble. Don't look yet. Have someone call them out to you, and see how well you can spell them.

accommodation	plausible
cemetery	recommend
connoisseur	regrettable
ecstasy	sacrilegious
hemorrhage	transferred
occurrence	unconscious
omission	withholding
permissible	zealot

6.3 What simple English sentence can you make from the following arrangement of words?

$\dfrac{\text{went}}{\text{I}}$	$\dfrac{\text{take}}{\text{to}}$	$\dfrac{\text{an}}{\text{-ly}}$	$\dfrac{\text{taking}}{\text{difficult}}$

Answer:

I underwent to undertake an overly difficult undertaking. (This requires spatial as well as verbal acuity.)

6.4 What does each word in the following list have in common: burst, calmness, panoply, weighing, student, abcess, hijack, definite

Answer:

They all have three consecutive letters of the alphabet.

6.5 Here are segments of English words. Can you identify words from which these segments could have been taken? (The letter order has not been changed.)

mphy	ysf
eupp	xpa
useo	lytr
owfl	oaut

Possible Answers:

emphysema	dysfunction
comeuppance	taxpayer
nauseous	flytrap
snowflake	coauthor

Puzzles like these cannot always be answered correctly right away, so don't get discouraged. Language improvement takes not only time and exercise, but carefully targeted stimulation. For example, if you have been exercising your brain's linguistic comprehension circuits, you cannot expect that your *spelling* will be improved. Moreover, verbal puzzles sometimes require that you use several kinds of brain function, so you may find it difficult to solve them because you're thinking in strictly linguistic mode when you need to be flexible enough to switch modes (as with question 6.4 above, which requires you to think of the physical relation of the words to each other as well as their meaning). So read on, relax, and get ready to stimulate *all* the parts of your brain.

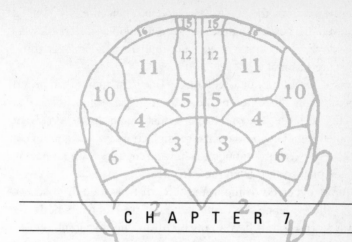

C H A P T E R 7

Improving Your Brain's Memory

One summer during high school I billed myself as a memory expert for the talent contest at my youth group camp. I wasn't showing off any special innate ability: My dad had given me a book on memory improvement about two months before the camp, and I wanted to try out what I had learned.

I spoke into the microphone and shivered as I heard my strange voice amplified through the sound system. I asked my fellow campers in the audience to provide me with a list of twenty-five words—called out one at a time—on which they could later question me: "What was word five? Word sixteen?" And so on.

Well, I got every word correct except one. I still remember it: It was item number seventeen, and the word was "announcements." The thing was, we all hated the various and lengthy announcements most always given by the adults. We hated announcements so much, we had even learned a song that referred to them as a horrible way to die, and we would sing it as an act of mild antagonism every time anyone started to make one.

I was miserable about forgetting the one item, rather than proud of remembering the other twenty-four. You can think of various reasons for my lapse. The one I favor is that, being shy, I didn't want to do something that would elicit a rousing chorus of the announcements song. It was hard enough to show off my trick without having to face any provocation from the audience.

It never occurred to me at the time that my memory had not failed me; the evidence says that just the reverse had happened. The word was stored somewhere in my brain, and my social inhibitions prevented me from retrieving it. The strength of those social inhibitions and the fact that they focused on the socially most arousing item tell me that they, not my memory, were the problem. It was a form of interference.

Certain lapses as well as triumphs of memory are not quite what they seem. Take Shereshevskii, the Russian mnemonics performer, who had a fantastic memory which relied heavily on imagery. There seemed to be no limit to the amount he could commit to memory. Where most of us would be happy to remember a simple shopping list, he could remember lists of more than one hundred digits, long strings of nonsense syllables (which are more difficult than meaningful words of comparable length), poetry in languages he did not know, complex figures, and elaborate scientific formulas.

Shereshevskii had an amazing capacity for *synesthesia*, a mixing of the senses in which one type of stimulation will evoke the sensation of another. Most people can do this to some extent: You might associate a low-pitched sound with subdued colors and a high-pitched sound with bright hues. You might also talk of the "blues" to describe a mood. But if you had asked Shereshevskii to describe a high tone, he might have replied as he did once: "It looks something like fireworks tinged with a pink-red hue. The strip of color feels rough and unpleasant, and it has an ugly taste—rather like that of a briny pickle. . . ."

Shereshevskii, a journalist, had been referred to Alexander Luria, a noted Russian psychologist, when his editor noticed that he never needed to take notes, no matter how complex the instructions for a story assignment. If the editor questioned him about his understanding of the instructions, Shereshevskii could repeat them word for word.

Luria tried out a test on Shereshevskii that would be beyond the pale for most of us mortals. He asked him to memorize an extremely complex, meaningless formula, part of which is given below:

$$N. \sqrt{d^2 . x\frac{85.}{vx}} \sqrt{\frac{276^2 . 86x.n^2b}{n^2v . \pi264}}$$

To do this, Shereshevskii concocted a story around the contents of the formula: "Neiman (N) came out and jabbed the ground with his cane (.). He looked at a dried-up tree which reminded him of a root ($\sqrt{}$), and he thought, 'it is no wonder that this tree withered and that its roots were lain bare, seeing that it was already standing when I built these two houses (d^2), and again he poked with his cane (.). He said, 'The houses are old, I'll have to get rid of them (x).' This gives a great return on his original capital; he invested 85,000 roubles in building them. The roof finishes off the building (—), and down below a man is standing and playing a harmonica (the x). . . ."

This strange story not only helped Shereshevskii remember the formula when he was tested right then, but fifteen years later, as well, when he was still able to recall the correct formula!

Although he was an impressive fellow, his memory wasn't much different from yours or mine at least in one respect. I mean this in all seriousness. Shereshevskii may have been quite facile (and well-practiced!) at using memory devices—his story technique is a well-known mnemonic tool—and he may have had an extraordinary ability to derive sensory impressions of the things he was planning to remember, but his memory per se seems to have worked like any other human memory. By understanding how to use mnemonic devices, and by implementing them in our daily routines, we too can improve the memory formation and retrieval functions of our brains—if not to quite the same degree Shereshevskii did.[1]

HOW MEMORY WORKS

Storage in the Brain

Research into the operations of memory has been likened to an attempt to break into a major bank vault using a toothpick. It is quite difficult to do this research, because we do not have ready access to the brains doing the memorizing. Moreover, those who have access to brains often get them only after the owners have died and can no longer display their memories. Even when human brains can be probed, there are few tests that reveal anything significant about how human memory operates.

Much of what we do know about human memory came from the probes performed by neurosurgeon Wilder Penfield on his epilepsy patients. When Penfield touched the electric probe to certain memory circuits, the patients would recall scenes, voices, or music. Penfield thought he was tapping into a "stream of a former consciousness flowing again," and his electrode really did seem to elicit a record of experiences. For example, when Penfield touched his electrode to a spot on the side of the brain of one patient, she suddenly said, "I think I heard a mother calling her little boy somewhere. It seemed to be something that happened years ago . . . in the neighborhood where I live." When he touched the probe to the same part of the brain eighteen minutes later, she said, "Yes, I hear the same familiar sounds. It seems to be a woman calling—the same lady. That was not in the neighborhood. It seemed to be at the lumberyard." The woman added, however, that she had never in her life been around a lumberyard.

Penfield's patients may not be reliving a past experience so much as constructing one based on memory fragments.[2] This is a lot like dreams in which the actual content is built up from experiences that follow a logic outside of your conscious experience. Memories get into the brain, but exactly how they are stored and how we retrieve them is still a mystery.

Fortunately, however, the chemical and structural processes of memory storage are getting less mysterious. We now know that when information from our experiences gets into the brain, nerve cells begin to adapt. Those nerve cells then act in different ways the next time information is transmitted through them. For example, they may transmit chemical information slower or faster. If an inhibitory circuit gets slower, there is less inhibition over time. Of course, whether inhibition is beneficial or detrimental to an overall function depends on the specific contribution of that circuit to the function. Our brains are thus physically changed by memory.

I was privileged to conduct a memory experiment with colleagues at the University of Southwestern Louisiana. We were aware that the experience of being handled (tamed) changes the way rodents (and many other animals) behave. This could only mean that the animals develop a "memory" of the handling experience as they are conditioned to it. We found that the trace metal nutrient content of their brains changes as the memory develops. Since human brains use trace metals in similar ways, we concluded that some aspects of memory formation change the way brains acquire and use dietary nutrients in chemical transmission.

Our memories seem to be housed in brains in a hierarchical way that could be likened to Chinese boxes. Some aspects of memory seem to be stored all over the brain, in no one location. But we also have memories that relate to our individual brain functions (e.g., language). These seem to be housed in the brain wherever the functions are located.

The anatomy of the brain's various memory functions can be readily observed in people who have had a small amount of brain damage from a stroke or surgery. If the damage occurred in certain language circuits, they cannot seem to remember words they are trying to say. They can construct words and parts of words from fragments recorded elsewhere, but their vocabulary storage seems to be lost. If the damage occurred in certain visual circuits, they may walk around bumping into things as if they are blind to the spatial features of the world. Their eyes can still record the visual world, but their brains are not able to make sense out of what is recorded.

Memory is a part of each of your brain's functions. When you exercise an individual function, what you are really doing is reinforcing its memory for the way it naturally performs. Professor Cameron Camp of the University of New Orleans says that memorized items become more retrievable the more you try to retrieve them.

This is probably because the stimulated brain circuit communicates with other areas of the brain that need to know about the added memory—the extra communication is a natural consequence of the brain's interconnections. Thus, brain exercise not only improves the function receiving the workout, but it also stimulates other areas of the brain connected to the exercised circuit.

Types of Memory

You have different ways of storing experiences that depend on the length of time you need to remember them. If you are relatively new to the corporation, and you meet a vice president for the first time, you may want to have her name firmly embedded in your psyche for easy retrieval. However, if you are ordering a pizza over the phone, and someone looks up the number and calls it out to you, you only have to remember the number for the time it takes to dial it. While you are reading this sentence, you have to hold the first phrase in storage long enough to finish the sentence so you can understand what I said.

Our memories have at least three distinct stages. Information must pass through all of them to be remembered for more than about half a minute.[3]

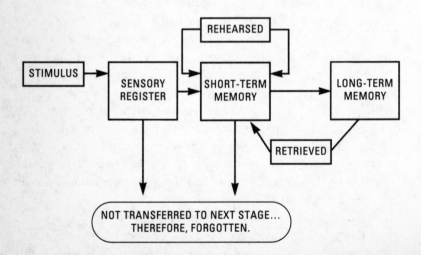

The first stage is a *sensory memory*. Whenever you see or hear something, a quick record of it gets stored in your sensory system. You know exactly what I mean if you have ever watched someone play with a sparkler or penlight in the dark. As the light source is waved around in the dark, you see the squiggly light line being drawn in space. In fact, what you see is your sensory memory of the light source, because the light itself has moved by the time you register it. In fact, once the light is turned off, there will be a brief moment when you still see its image glowing in the dark—this is memory at work. Sensory memory decays quickly unless you can get it into the second kind of memory called *short-term memory*.

Short-term memory has been equated with the conscious mind, because it usually holds the contents of your attention. According to memory expert Elizabeth Loftus, short-term memory cannot hold its contents for more than a half-minute or so. But you can keep information in short-term memory simply by continuing to pay attention to it. For example, as you continue to repeat a phone number to yourself, the constant attention to it keeps it in consciousness. As soon as you turn your attention to another matter—say, the toppings you want on your pizza—the phone number is lost to consciousness.

If, however, you are a pizza aficionado, and the phone number you have rings up the best place in town, its special importance might help you get it into long-term storage, especially if you repeat it several times or use a mnemonic aid. (Businesses often encourage the use of such memory aids by incorporating them into their numbers. If your pizza place wanted you to remember its number, it might arrange to get a number like 342-5743, so that it could then advertise for you to "DIAL PIE." The mnemonic device makes long-term memory an easier job.)

Long-term memory is the storage form we usually think of as memory. It holds all the data that have made you into the person you are today. It holds the memory of your piano recital, your vocabulary, your parents' faces, the knowledge of how to dress in the morning, as well as information about traffic laws when you drive.

The fact that you do not always think about the items in long-term storage only means that the system is efficient. Once you recall a piece of information from long-term storage, your present attention to it focuses the information in short-term memory. This means that the information is now back at the surface of conscious awareness, available for use. The multilayered construction of memory frees you from the weight of the huge number of items you add to storage every year.

Any attempt to exercise your memory will take advantage of the way it is constructed. With brain exercise, you will enlarge your ability to keep data in conscious storage, hasten the process of getting this information into long-term storage so that less of it gets lost, build your long-term storage capacity, and facilitate the recall—retrieval —of the memories you have stored. If this sounds difficult, keep in mind that you already have all these abilities and have been using them all your life. Memory exercise, like the exercise for any brain or body function, is simply a matter of improving on what you already possess.

Amnesia

It is simply not possible to imagine life without memory. Our very identities are bound up with our memories. Every once in a while, you hear a strange story about a person being lost to his family because of a memory lapse that lasts for over a year. Steven Kubacki underwent such an ordeal in 1978. He had planned to go cross-country skiing, but got lost and tired. The next thing he remembered was waking up in a field and realizing it was spring. Fourteen months had passed since he had set out in Michigan, and he was now in Massachusetts. Somehow he had lost over a year of his life.

However sad and desperate a situation this was, it is clear that Steven Kubacki did not lose his memory entirely. He could still remember the basic facts about personhood: He knew he had to eat, clothe himself, find shelter, and talk to other people. He was not completely helpless, despite the fact that he had lost a large segment of his personal long-term memory. But memory loss can be much more radical than that. One of the well-known clinical cases is a fellow known to the world only by his initials: H.M. He underwent brain surgery to remove large brain segments on both sides that were causing him to have severe seizures. Before the surgery, he had no memory problems. Afterwards, he was no longer able to get anything from short-term memory into long-term storage. No one on the hospital staff was recognizable to him except for the doctor, whom he had known for years. If you introduced yourself to him, he could carry on a pleasant conversation, but if you left for a couple of hours and came back, he would not know who you were. He could remember everything that happened prior to the operation by retrieving information from long-term storage, and he could hold information in short-term memory long enough to carry on discourse, but he could not make new memories.

Fortunately, forgetting where you put your keys, what the name of the new vice president is, or who is the best supplier for a certain resource at your company are nowhere in the same league with these amnesias, nor do they suggest you might suffer one in the future. Excessive forgetting may cost you a promotion, but it does not threaten your identity, and it probably does not mean you are getting senile or suffering from a degenerative disease. However, it is important enough that you may want to do some of the exercises in this chapter to counteract it.

Forgetting

One reason people forget is that the *list* of things to remember *is too long*. Seven seems to be the magic number—the maximum number of items that most people are able to remember at any one time, if memory aids are not used. The more items you try to pay attention to—to hold in short-term memory—the more you will forget. One of the great experimental psychologists, Donald Hebb, touched on this problem when he thought he was losing his intellectual abilities at the tender age of forty-seven. He was reading a journal article directly relevant to his work, and he thought it would be a good idea to make a note in the margin about an important fact. He turned the page and was horrified to find a penciled note in his own handwriting. That he had not remembered reading the article at all suggested to him that his brain was undergoing an early (and rapid) deterioration.

But then he decided to take stock of things. He was chairman of a large academic department that was undergoing rebuilding. He had organized a new laboratory and was setting up an intensive research program, and he was carrying on a regular teaching load. On top of all that, one of his important books had just been published, and he had to read about twice as much to be responsive to the critical and evaluative duties that such a book brings. Hebb decided that he was simply doing too much. He started to relax and began to take time off for lunch. He also cut down on some of his load and became more selective in his reading material. Once he did this, he found that he had no more memory lapses and could remember whatever he wanted to.[4]

If you have seven things to do on a busy morning, and you add to your list in any way—major *or* minor—you put yourself at risk for forgetting. For example, suppose you walk in one morning, and your secretary says that you: (1) have to call Beverly in public relations, (2) must have the memo about marketing on the vice president's desk by ten and (3) have to contact a branch office about their lawsuit. Now suppose that before you take these messages into your office, you (4) put your car keys down on the secretary's filing cabinet while you stand chatting with him for a minute. Then the vice president walks over, tells you that "We have to talk," and ushers you immediately into your office. He tells you that: (5) the CEO is talking buyout with your major competitor, (6) it is your job to keep morale up among middle management, (7) he wants a review of the department budgets by tomorrow, and (8) he wants your opinion on the efficacy of an alternative marketing scheme that he will give you this afternoon.

I included the placement of your keys among the items that have to be held in short-term memory because the vice president's arrival interfered with your putting the keys where you usually put them, which is remembered in long-term memory. You also did not get to release your short-term memory by consolidating information into long-term memory or by writing list items down. Any time you begin to build a list this long, you put yourself at risk for forgetting, especially when the list contains items of mixed context—i.e., car keys and department budgets.

But there is another reason why you are likely to forget the keys. You tend to remember items at the beginning and end of any list. You are therefore more likely to remember to call Beverly, write the memo on marketing, review the budgets, and provide an opinion on the marketing than you are to remember where you put your keys. Later, when you cannot find your keys, there is no need to get frantic about impending senility. More likely explanations are (1) you simply have a lot on your mind (a long list of things to remember), and (2) the placement of the keys was in the middle of that list.

People also forget because of *interference*, which simply means that other associations may inhibit the thing to be remembered. Interference is of two basic kinds: proactive and retroactive. If you are new to the company, and you learn a particular marketing scheme right away, you might experience a little difficulty learning a different marketing scheme later, especially if you do not like it as much. When the memory of the earlier marketing scheme interferes with the later one, you have experienced proactive interference. If, however, you have switched companies, learned a new system, and someone has asked you for details about the old system, you might have trouble providing them. Once again, you have not fallen prey to some deadly brain disease. You are merely experiencing retroactive interference.

Motivated Forgetting

With insight into your own psychology, you can uncover many additional reasons for your forgetting important facts or events. For example, *motivated forgetting* may be the cause of Ted Kennedy's poor memory of the events that occurred during the accident at Chappaquiddick.[5] For several years following the accident, Kennedy maintained that he had no memory or recollection of the exact events. Although many have accused him of stonewalling, another process might have taken place: the tendency to forget things that are associated with great stress or pain.

It is commonplace among accident victims to forget the events surrounding a trauma. One of my brothers was involved in a head-on collision on the highway, and he does not remember anything about the crash or his hospital stay. New York's Central Park jogger is said to remember nothing of the brutal attack and rape that left her close to death. This kind of memory loss certainly has adaptive value. If you survive such a trauma, you would not want your brain to store the literal record of your pain and suffering for recall the next time you are on the highway, or jogging in the park. Better to forget than to live the pain all over again when you can least afford to do so.

Pain and stress do not have to be purely physical to make you forget. Psychologically meaningful events have great impact on what you remember and how you remember it. A painful divorce, the loss of a child, being abused by a loved one, or even losing your favorite pet can all leave their marks on your memory. It only takes the right stimulus to bring them out.

For example, take the scenario in chapter one about the vice president from a branch office dropping in to have a word with you. This was a frantic scene in which you could not for the life of you dredge up his name from your long-term memory. But now suppose this is a case of motivated forgetting, and that you realize the necessity to relax, sit back, and try to achieve insight into the hidden reason you are forgetting. You study his face, and it dawns on you that he looks like the obnoxious brother of the man you divorced eight months ago. With insight comes release. Your memory lapse was borne of an emotional interference. Once the interfering memory is removed by your insight, the original memory can be recalled.

As a professor I have taught many classes about brain science. The lectures that are most fun for me are the spontaneous ones in which a stream of consciousness gets released by an interesting question. On these occasions the lectures just flow out of memory. Time passes quickly, and the lecture hour is often up before I know it. Yet on one of these occasions I got stuck on a memory. I could not for the life of me recall what I wanted to say about a certain brain mechanism I knew quite well. I finally realized that I had originally learned this particular material during an emotionally up-setting period. The realization released the memory, and I stopped fumbling and got back in the groove of the lecture. It was not that I had forgotten the information, but it was necessary to release it from the emotional interference.

Aging and Senility

The older concept of aging was quite pessimistic. The assumption was that after a certain age—approximately thirty—you start to lose brain cells every day. You don't notice any loss of cognitive powers for awhile because of the inherent redundancy of brain cells that control a particular function. You can afford the losses—at first. As you get older, however, your cumulative losses are so great that they begin to have an impact on your cognitive abilities and memory. If you live long enough, it is inevitable that you will become senile. Those few senior citizens who escape this natural process are the extremely lucky, somehow beyond the reaches of objective scientific prediction.

Brain scientists now regard these predictions and assumptions as overly pessimistic. Marian Diamond has studied brains from rats of various ages and has found absolutely no truth to the notion that brain cells are lost in healthy, normal elderly animals. She was also able to study Einstein's brain, which had resided for years in a freezer behind a beer cooler in Kansas. In the brain from this extraordinary seventy-six-year-old, Diamond found an above average number of cells that support and nourish the brain's nerve cells. Aging does not necessarily mean deterioration. People who become senile have, for one reason or another, some form of degenerative brain process. If you do not get this organic disease—and the majority of older people do not—you are likely to remain alert and capable of improving your brain functions while you age.

Although aging decreases (but does not eliminate) one kind of neural plasticity—the number of nerve connections fashioned by the brain during memory formation—the actual chemical processes of memory in the remaining nerve connections are not impaired. Significant memory loss only occurs when the aging person has a real form of brain deterioration such as Alzheimer's disease. In fact, research shows that memories of people over 60 may in many cases be more accurate than those of younger people. When almost fifteen hundred people classified in three age groups—below 60, 60–69, and 70 or older—were asked to supply memorized information that could be verified independently, a high degree of accuracy among people over 60 was found. For certain kinds of information (e.g., make and year of automobile), people over 70 were just as accurate as those under 60.[6]

Memory loss, previously considered an intrinsic part of the aging process, may really be due to other extrinsic factors. Scientists J. W. Rowe and R. L. Kahn believe that the role of aging in cognitive deficits has been overstated, because gerontological research tends to neglect the substantial variation in any group of older individuals.[7] They suggest that the memory decline in aging could be due to relatively simple factors such as a lack of intellectual stimulation.

In essence, your beliefs can make you your own worst enemy. If you believe in your eventual deterioration, you are almost certain to make this a self-fulfilling prophecy by neglecting to get the intellectual stimulation you need to keep mentally fit.

The many examples of towering intellectual achievement in the latter half of life belie any fears that to age is to decline. "It is not Shakespeare's early plays that are most highly thought of," as Donald Hebb has told us; "there is no way you can explain *Macbeth* as the product of fading intelligence propped up by a bigger store of information."[8] Hebb also reminds us that Immanuel Kant's *Critique of Pure Reason* appeared when he was 57. Of course, Agatha Christie was turning out choice murder mysteries when she was in her 70s and 80s, and Robert Heinlein, two years before his death from heart failure in 1988, published *The Cat Who Walks Through Walls*; he was 79 at the time. Margaret Mead, the anthropologist, was also quite intellectually active when she was in her 70s. You no doubt have your own favorite, but the point is that the content of your memory and intellect is mostly up to you. Normal aging need not put an end to mental growth.

GAMES AND EXERCISES TO STIMULATE YOUR BRAIN'S MEMORY ABILITY

Before You Think You Have Forgotten

The fact is that interference is a more powerful cause of forgetting than simple decay. Sometimes the forgetting occurs when the new is unable to compete successfully with the old (proactive inter-ference); alternatively, sometimes the old gives way to the new (retroactive interference). Even more powerful is the kind of psychological interference that may shield us from painful memories—motivated forgetting—even if those memories are not so traumatic as those Ted Kennedy or the Central Park jogger would have to face. When you have a memory lapse, the first thing to keep in mind is whether something might be interfering with your record or retrieval. This first exercise is designed to help you become more sensitive to the possible reasons for various memory lapses.

> Bring to mind three memory lapses that you have had. If you cannot remember any (no pun intended), simply write them down as you come across them. Then, for each lapse, write down a few details of the setting in which it occurred, and a possible reason why it occurred. This exercise will not help you unless you are honest with yourself and are not afraid to list possible psychological reasons as well as "simple" ones such as "in the middle of a long list."

When Memories Are Not Lost

In a biological system such as the brain, some memory decay is inevitable. This is because the various proteins and other biochemical constituents of memory undergo constant decay and breakdown. Information stored there can eventually be lost if the chemicals are not continually replenished. However, the fact that biological chemicals can be degraded, and the information in them lost, does not necessarily mean the total loss of a memory.

Brains have several ways of performing their functions, and it is likely that memories are built from several fragments pieced together in the brain. Thus, even if certain storage proteins are lost, some memory will be retained. It is like having a complex jigsaw puzzle with a few pieces missing. As more of the pieces are removed, the picture becomes less and less distinct, but you can usually manage to perceive the whole even with several pieces missing.

The first psychologist to study memory experimentally, Hermann Ebbinghaus, proved approximately a century ago that even if you are not aware of retaining a memory, it may still be coded somewhere in your mind. This has been validated in studies showing that relearning material takes much less time than learning it for the first time (the principle of *savings upon relearning*). This can only hold true because some material has in fact been retained and is retrievable.

In fact, many memorized items may not be lost at all—though difficulties in retrieving them may make you feel otherwise. When I first sat down to write this chapter, I was quite fuzzy about the specifics of my opening anecdote. After all, the event had occurred almost twenty years ago, and I had not thought about the details in the meantime. Although I easily remembered the one item I had "forgotten" at the time, I was not sure I could remember the memory system I had been using. However, as I started thinking more about memory, I remembered the first nine memory system peg words I had used (more on this later). As of this writing, I cannot recall any peg words from the next ten or twenty on the list, but I know I would recognize them if I saw them, and they certainly would be easy to "relearn."

This brings up the next exercise whose purpose is to show that your memory is not all that bad.

Recall from your school days a poem, sonnet, or speech that you memorized. If one does not come readily to mind, do not place a quick (negative) value judgment on your memory. Close your eyes, relax, and "let it flow." It could be part of the Gettysburg Address, the Preamble to the Constitution, a Shakespearean soliloquy, Coleridge's "Kubla Khan," or Emily Dickinson's "Because I could not stop for death—." Relax once again and remember that you are not being graded on this exercise. Try to remember the setting in which you first learned or recited the lines. Once you have put yourself in the scene, try to remember the feelings that were stirred by the words. Was it *pleasure* when you recited it from memory the first time for your parents? Did you have an aesthetic feeling for the words, or were you perhaps aroused by the power of them?

If you have been able to go this far, now try to write down some of the words that made you feel the way you did. You are doing well if you are able to write down anything.

Now look up the piece. Read it and let your memories flood back into you. If you remembered your feelings about it correctly, you will probably feel the same ones. Recognition should bring you an additional source of pleasure, and it should also tell you that no matter how much you think you have forgotten, you still have these ancient memories lurking in your brain. If you like, you can rememorize the piece. It should not take long, given the strength of your previous memory.

Creatures of Habit

James Reason and Klara Mycielska ask whether you have ever said "Thank you" to a vending machine, or gone into your bedroom to prepare for bed, only to change clothes for another outing?[9] They also remind us of this slip from the old children's word game:

Q: What do you call the tree that grows from an acorn?
A: Oak.
Q: What do you call a funny story?
A: Joke.
Q: What do you call the sound made by a frog?
A: Croak.
Q: What do you call the white of an egg?
A: ———.

Of course, the answer is "albumin," but newcomers to the game usually say "yolk" as a slip of habit. The word game induces the wrong response by using powerful habitual word associations (memories) (e.g., you always say egg yolk and rarely egg albumin) and a rhyming scheme that pulls you into the response. I mention these inducers because they are not unlike the ones that cause you to make everyday slips of habit. For example, our dog's leash and her treats are kept in the same closet. When I go to take her for a walk, I sometimes reach into the closet without thinking and pull out a dog treat. Both retrieval behaviors are a matter of habit. When I do not think about it, or I am thinking about food, one habit becomes more of an inducer.

The next exercise is planned to give you insight into these memory lapses. Armed with insight, you are less likely to embarrass yourself when you can least afford it.

> Take a few minutes and jot down five of your daily habits, complete with the routine behaviors used in the performance of each habit. Take care to note the time of the day these habits are normally performed.
>
> Then, for the next several days, keep a record of any slips of habit you make. Try to tie them to these daily routines that you have written down. If you find that the slips occur during routines you have *not* written down, you are developing evidence that your insights into your habits are purging you of memory slips. If this is the case, write down another five of your daily routines and continue to keep a record of your lapses. By gaining insight into all your daily habits, you may be able to purge yourself of the slips.

Tying Faces to Names

Three basic problems occur when you try to tie names to faces:[10] (1) You may not have much *time*. If you are introduced briefly to the members of the board, and the chairperson wants to get on with "real" business, it may be difficult to make all the associations necessary to moving the name from short-term to long-term storage. (2) Some *names* are harder to *encode* than others. You may not have trouble thinking of associations with names like Hill, Armstrong,

Tower, or Bell, but think about what you would do if you met a person with a name like mine: Chafetz. (3) Faces may provide meaningful visual (and spatial) information, but they do not provide a meaningful verbal pattern. You will need to perform special *face encoding*.

One way to remember faces and names is to use a *distinctive feature* of a person's face to help recall the name. That feature should then be linked with a clever encoding of the name. For example, suppose you are introduced to Mary Pickford. You think carefully about her face while you introduce yourself. You may wish to enlarge some features or minimize others much as a caricature artist does. In your case, however, you are trying to emphasize those features that fit with your distortion of her name. One way to do this for someone named Mary Pickford might be to think how closely her eyebrows are *married* to the *Ford pick*up truck of a nose she has. (Your new acquaintance need never know how unflattering are the associations you use to remember her name.)

> As an exercise in name distortion, I will list 11 names chosen semirandomly from literature. Your job is to distort them into easily remembered code words that you could associate with particular facial features.
>
> Jake Barnes
> Edna Pontellier
> Emma Bovary
> Colonel Aureliano Buendia
> Augie March
> Alexander Portnoy
> Billy Pilgrim
> Willy Loman
> Daisy Miller
> Constance Chatterley
> Amanda Wingfield

It is not hard to distort names, once you get the hang of it, and the practice is certainly fun. However, you also need practice in tying names to faces. One way to do this is to use people you already know.

Write down the names of eight friends, relatives, or public figures whose faces are well known to you. Use the name and face distortion technique in an attempt to remember the faces and names as if you were meeting these people for the first time.

1.

2.

3.

4.

5.

6.

7.

8.

Keep in mind that when you tie names to faces, you are exercising several functional areas of your brain. A memory for faces depends on spatial recognition abilities and therefore exercises brain cells and fibers that deal in spatial information processing. The memory of names depends upon language functions, and the linking of the two depends upon several interconnecting circuits. Large areas of your brain are needed for face–name memory and are exercised every time you attempt it.

Filling in the Gaps

Our lives are filled with periods of waiting—for buses, taxis, theater seats, bank lines, et cetera—in which we let our minds wander. These are perfect occasions to squeeze in some brain exercise. You can perform many of the following exercises during such times. Even if you cannot record the results, you can always do the exercise and write down your results later.

Locations

This exercise is suggested by memory expert Alan Baddeley.[11] Like many of the mnemonic aids, it depends on an active visualizing of spatial relations.

> Think of ten locations in your home. You should choose them in a natural sequence. For example, one sequence would include locations you would automatically see as you approach your front door, enter the front room, and proceed through the house to your bedroom. You should check to see if you can consistently identify the same ten locations in your mental procession throughout the home. Now, whenever you have up to ten things on a list to memorize (if you have more, you can always add to the number of locations), imagine a scenario in which they are placed in these various locations.
>
> For this exercise, I will provide two lists of ten things to memorize. I will walk you through my mental home for the first list. The second list is for your mental home.

First	Second
car	book
blinds	lion
cat	shelf
string	xylophone
prisoner	postage
violet	candidate
newspaper	Swiss cheese
tree	helium
light	apple
toys	word

Here is one way the first ten items could be placed in locations in my mental home: An exquisite *car* is propped up on my front porch, preventing entry through the front door. Nevertheless, I open the front door, only to be confronted with a set of *blinds*. I am able to walk through the blinds only if I twist the control rod, which I do. As I enter the living room, a large Persian *cat* is resting on my sofa. The cat is as large as the sofa and I am annoyed that it is shedding all over the sofa. I decide to go to my bedroom upstairs. I have difficulty getting to the hallway where the stairs are because of the large ball of *string* the cat has been playing with. I open the door to the stairwell, only to find a *prisoner* sitting in his prison suit on the stairs. He wishes me well and asks how my day has been. I go up the stairs, only to find that an African *violet* has been placed at the top of the stairs. I think the prisoner must have put it there, but he claims to be color blind and to know nothing of violets. A *newspaper* has been thrown through the first dormer window, which I will now have to replace. I knew I should have uprooted the *tree* I saw growing in the front yard this morning, because it has grown through the second dormer window. I open my dresser, only to find that residual *light* is left over from an old Bud Light commercial. On my bed are all my favorite *toys* from childhood.

Well, it worked for me, and I hope it will for you, too. After writing this, I tried to see if I could remember the items from the first list, and it was no problem. For those of you who would point out that I selected those items to begin with, and that I should therefore have a good memory of them, I should mention that I also picked the items on the second list. It has rolled off my computer screen as of my writing of this paragraph, and I find that I cannot remember more than five words on it.

If you have any trouble remembering the items on my first list after reading my story, it is not because you are having difficulty with this memory technique. You are only experiencing the difference between passive and active memorization. It is a lot easier when you compose your *own* story on your *own* list.

I should also mention that during the normal course of my writing I edit my daily output the next morning. Before I edited this section, I tested my memory of the first list by recalling all the items in order. It was no problem. I could visualize the car propped up on my front porch, the blinds as I walked in, and I even had a good laugh at the huge cat sitting on my imaginary sofa. The rest of the list was equally vivid. Once you memorize a list, it should not be difficult to keep it in storage at least until you can use it the next day. Imagine how useful this can be when you need to remember to take several things to your client the next day, but you have nothing on you with which to write them down.

Language Tools

You can use most of your brain's abilities to facilitate your memory. For example, in the preceding exercises you used your spatial abilities to link items you wanted to remember with visual images, thereby creating a mnemonic device that fixed the items more firmly in your mind. Other mental functions can also be used to assist memory. Language ability, for example, can be helpful, particularly for those who are verbal in orientation. One of the old standbys is to take the first letter of each to-be-remembered item and string the letters together into something recognizable or coherent. Many of you are acquainted with the BIV family, especially their famous son, ROY G BIV, whose name letters are the first letters of the colors in the visible spectrum (red, orange, yellow, green, blue, indigo, and violet). The language aid I used for learning the cranial nerves of the head and neck was: On Old Olympus's Towering Top A Finn And German Viewed Some Hops. Each first letter corresponds to the first letter of each cranial nerve (olfactory, optic, oculomotor, trochlear, trigeminal, abducens, facial, acoustic, glossopharyngeal, vagus, spinal accessory, and hypoglossal). By the way, I wrote this from memory; the memory aid really worked.

One of the country's foremost experts on memory, Alan Baddeley, tells an amusing anecdote about how he misremembered a language aid for remembering the value of *pi* to the first twenty decimal places.[12] He had thought the mnemonic was based on a rhyming scheme, but in fact it was the length of the words used to remember the digits. Since most of you have access to calculators or computers (and little need to calculate with *pi*), I haven't a clue what you could use this particular mnemonic for, but it is a good example of a way to remember numbers:

Pie

> I wish I could determine pi
> Eureka cried the great inventor
> Christmas pudding Christmas pie
> Is the problem's very centre

The number of letters in each word gives the value of *pi*: 3.14159265358979323846.

FOR this exercise, invent a language mnemonic to remember the first or second list in the preceding section. For example, the first list can be remembered by the following sentence that uses the first letter of each to-be-remembered word:

Cathy blurted, "Crazy stringers play violins nigh three long terms."

Peg Words

Many memory experts like this method. This was the method I used during my summer camp talent show (though I used a slightly different version than the one presented here).

Compare memory to a large, floorless storage room or garage. Since new information cannot be stacked on the floor of a floorless room, it must be hung on pegs on the walls. Once you have created mental pegs, you can hang information on them by using imagery. Imagery works exactly as before, when you took a walk through your mental house.

Pegs can be fashioned in many ways, but one of the easiest is to use a rhyming scheme with words:

1 = bun	2 = gnu	3 = tree
4 = door	5 = hive	6 = sticks
7 = heaven	8 = grate	9 = wine
10 = hen		

Once you have these pegs in place, you can tie information to them easily. The next exercise takes advantage of this peg method to help you remember what to take to your deposition at a law firm across town.

You are an associate attorney at a large law firm. You are having a phone conversation with your supervising law partner, but you are at a booth and have nothing to write with. You decide to use the peg method to remember what she wants you to take to your deposition. She is in a hurry and rapidly requests that you take: her notary stamp, a calculator, the plastic model used by the expert witness, a tape recorder, the Sacco and Vanzetti brief, her briefcase, the Rockford file, all pleadings, the previous deposition, and notepaper.

You are usually reliable, so she does not ask whether you have got it all down. However, using the peg word method, you should have no trouble. See if you can place these ten items on your memory pegs within two to three minutes. An example follows:

The gun is stamped with a notary seal. A very smart gnu is using her horns to calculate on the calculator. The plastic model is caught in the knee joint. A huge tape recorder is on the floor, recording everything you say. Sacco and Venzetti are going for a nice, long drive. Her briefcase is where she keeps her bag of tricks. The Rockford file has gone to heaven. Don't let the pleadings slip through the grate. The previous deposition smells like pine. You could certainly use a three-foot pen to write on the notepaper.

Almost any systematic scheme can be used to create peg words. For example, the alphabet can be used to create twenty-six peg words. The following are my choices for alphabet peg words. If you find that a different peg word comes more easily to mind for any letter, it is better to use it because your memory will benefit from an easier recall of that cue word.

A = hay	B = bee	C = sea	D = deed
E = eat	F = effort	G = jeep	H = hatch
I = eye	J = (blue) jay	K = cave	L = el or ell
M = Auntie Em	N = end	O = oaf	P = pea
Q = cue	R = art	S = ess	T = tea
U = ewe	V = veal	W = whew!	X = ex
Y = white	Z = zzzzz		

A few explanations: L = an elevated train or the wing of a building; M = Auntie Em, as in Dorothy and Toto; S = as in an ess curve on the highway; W = whew, as in great relief; X = an ex-spouse; and Z = catching a few z's.

Chunking

Chunking may be one of the brain's natural functions. Whenever you study something that is complicated or otherwise has a lot of information, your mind attempts to make sense of it by trying to put the information into patterns. By enhancing this natural tendency, you can become more facile at remembering long strings of items.

A previous example was actually one type of chunking. When you took the first letter of each visible color and turned it into ROY G BIV, you reduced 7 items of information into an easily remembered 3 by grouping the items into a pattern. However, to get a feel for a purer form of chunking, try to remember the following list of digits. When you have studied the list for a minute, close your eyes and see if you can repeat all the digits in turn:

1, 4, 9, 2, 1, 9, 8, 4, 1, 7, 7, 6, 1, 8, 1, 2

If you tried to learn each digit by itself, you no doubt had trouble remembering all 16 of them within your minute's memory period. After all, the number of digits is longer (by over twice) than the 6 to 7 easily remembered under normal circumstances. However, my previous statements might have primed you into performing some chunking of the digits. If you looked at the digits as a series of 4 easily recognizable dates—1492, 1984, 1776, 1812—you would have had no trouble remembering all 16 of them. Chunking reduces the information you have to remember and relates it to something already recognizable in your memory.

Not every list of numbers, however, has easily recognizable chunks. Sometimes it is necessary to force the patterns into chunks that are convenient for your personal use. For example, look at the following numbers:

1, 8, 0, 9, 5, 3, 6, 1, 2, 0

A personalized chunking might go something like this: 180 is the number of seconds in a 3-minute egg; 95 is the age of a very old person; 36 is my age; 120 characters per second is the speed of my printer.

The more you do this, the better at it you will become. You only have to try it a few times to get the hang of it. To give you an opportunity to practice, I will provide 3 lists of random numbers below. Take 3 to 5 minutes for each list. Write down the chunks you develop. As you get used to forming chunks, you will begin to see patterns in other kinds of lists that will help you learn information at breathtaking speed.

1, 0, 2, 7, 5, 3, 9, 6, 2, 3, 7, 1
9, 1, 7, 6, 2, 1, 6, 4, 6, 4, 2, 0, 8, 0
3, 3, 7, 5, 7, 2, 2, 2, 0, 6

CHECK YOUR PROGRESS

Keep a diary of your progress through the following memory exercises (as well as all the exercises in this book). You will want memory sharpness to become a habit, and you will need a record of your progress with each memory technique and test.

TODAY'S LISTS

7.1.   As you continue to learn new things by using mnemonic devices, your memory will improve as you become more facile with acquiring information. For this first progress check, use a mnemonic device to memorize the ten most important things you have to do today. Do not write them down unless you feel that forgetting one will ruin relations with your firm—or someone near and dear to you. If it is important to write them down, try not to look at the list but instead rely on your memory.

7.2. Next time you go shopping, use a mnemonic device to memorize the shopping list. As before, go ahead and write it down if you have to, but try not to look at the list while you are shopping.

7.3. Next time you go to a party, use a mnemonic device to remember all the names of people you meet. Be sure to greet everyone by name and to use their names at least once during the course of the evening.

NEW INFORMATION

7.4. Use a mnemonic device to memorize ten bits of information from the morning paper. Write them down, and see if you remember them when you get home in the evening.

HISTORICAL INFORMATION

7.5. Use a mnemonic device to memorize historical information. Set a goal of memorizing a list of historical information three times a week. Possible lists: the presidents, the wars, the bestsellers for the past year, Oscar winners for the best film for the past fifteen years, et cetera.

RANDOM INFORMATION

7.6. Memorize the titles of the books on your shelf.

7.7. Memorize the titles of the records, tapes, and/or CDs in your collection.

COMBINING MEMORY FUNCTIONS WITH OTHER BRAIN FUNCTIONS

7.8. Memorize a favorite poem or passage from a favorite book or document.

7.9. Memorize the street plan in an unfamiliar section of town.

7.10. Draw the following objects from memory:

your watch face
your front door or the front of your house
position of furniture in your office

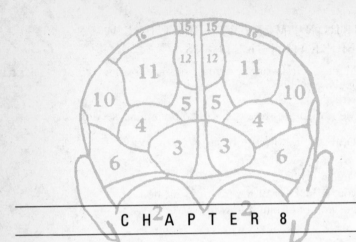

CHAPTER 8

Your Logical Brain

In my favorite children's book, *The Phantom Tollbooth* by Norton Juster, our hero—a little boy named Milo—suddenly finds that he and his traveling companions are whisked away to a strange place after making remarks that each of them had considered innocuous. They meet a fellow who they decide must be called Canby, because he is both as smart and as stupid as *can be*. Canby tells them they are on the Island of Conclusions and that they had better make themselves at home, because they are likely to be there for some time. When asked how they got there, he explains, "You jumped. . . . That's the way most everyone gets here. It's really quite simple: Every time you decide something without having a good reason, you jump to Conclusions whether you like it or not." He also tells them that it is not so easy getting back, because you can never jump away from conclusions. To get back, you have to swim in the Sea of Knowledge, which most people can do and still come out completely dry.

Logic is a fact of human life, but almost any animal with a decent-size brain can commit a logical fallacy. My dog has learned that she gets a treat when she sits on command. In the winter, when the space heater shuts off after reaching the setpoint temperature, she will go and sit in front of it until it turns on again. After all, the act of sitting usually gets her what she wants, and the heater will turn on again if she sits long enough.

Although it is easy to laugh at the poor creature who doesn't know any better, it is no laughing matter when the managing director tells you to run an advertising campaign exactly like the one that was successful for his dad fifteen years ago. Never mind that the times are different and that any number of critical factors have changed. *He* knows what is successful and what is not.

SUPERSTITIOUS BEHAVIOR

Research in the field of psychology has uncovered an important principle of illogical behavior. Behavioral scientists have found that if an interval of time elapses between what you do to attain a goal and the actual fulfillment of that goal, and during that interval you engage in some other kinds of activity, you are likely to tie those secondary, irrelevant behaviors to the outcome. This is called a superstitious belief, because the fact is that what you did has no real relation to what later occurred.

Superstitious behavior can occur in any facet of life, but it is especially apparent during certain sports activities. Most of us are familiar with the bowler who contorts his or her body, jumps up and down, or does a little dance while the ball is en route. The only factor that affects the way the ball strikes the pins is the manner in which it was released. However, if body language precedes a strike, it will no doubt be used again, no matter how illogical it is to see a cause and effect connection between the fall of the pins and the bowler's contortions. That's just human nature—and animal nature, too, as my dog's behavior indicates.

Superstitious behavior is in fact so animal-like that much of the early research on it was done on pigeons. The pigeons were given a reward every fifteen seconds regardless of what they were doing at the time. The pigeons could be bowing, cooing, or walking about in a particular spot in the cage. Whatever they were doing just before the reward was likely to be done again before the next reward. For example, if a bird had walked to the east corner of the cage, bowed, cooed, and turned around, it would perform the exact sequence of behaviors right before the next reward. The animals connected their behavior to the outcome. Since the behavior and the outcome were not connected in any causal way, such behavior is called "superstitious."

Office politics are often based on similar bits of nonlogic. Take for example a project that depends upon multiple contributions for its success. Johnny Hot-shot's contribution may not be any more important than yours—in fact may be considerably less important —but if he's observed working late immediately before the successful launch of the project, the project director may give a disproportionate share of the credit to Johnny, even if his late night actions consisted of nothing more than scribbling on a worksheet. Behaviors that are in evidence before a big success are associated with that success.

The same principle works in reverse, too. Suppose that you are observed working late prior to the launch of a big project and the project then flops: You could get blamed as if you were the cause of the failure, especially if the project director has developed other superstitions about who is responsible for the successes in your particular company.

The sad thing about this scenario is that the mental operations that are victimizing you are not superior to those my dog engages in when she sits in front of the space heater in an effort to turn it on.

STATISTICAL REASONING

This exercise will help you learn a logic to prevent a special case of overgeneralizing. Research has shown that once people understand this reasoning, they are better at applying it successfully to all sorts of situations.

The logic involves a statistical notion about large numbers. It applies whenever there is uncertainty in a situation in which results can be measured. If I ask you to test a coin that may be unfairly weighted, you would certainly like to flip it more than a few times to be able to tell. If the discrepancy is slight (the uncertainty is high), you will want to flip it a great number of times. However, if the discrepancy is so great that you can practically tell by picking up the coin, you don't need to flip it as many times.

Most people can apply this statistical reasoning to inanimate objects like coins. The difficulty in using it comes when you are judging other people. If you are not aware of bypassing statistical reasoning, you are more likely to jump to conclusions about the whole domain from a small sample of behavior.

In this exercise, scenarios are provided in which conclusions have to be drawn. Your job is to analyze those conclusions according to the logic of large numbers. Sample analyses are provided below.

—The food is not as good the second time you go to a restaurant, where on your first visit you thought the food was fantastic.

—Your new employee was given a raise almost immediately because of his stellar performance, but he seems to have slacked off.

—Your new employee is not as good as she was during the interview.

—A performer turns out to be a star when you thought she was about average during the audition.

—Your spouse takes up a new hobby and you are not impressed with the first few efforts.

Analyses

The restaurant: Any performance—including the preparation of food—has variability. The more variability there is, the more uncertainty you have. You will need much more than one sample to draw a conclusion about the domain of foods served by that restaurant. Arguments that restaurants have a high turnover of chefs or cooks miss the point.

New employee #1: You need more than one small sample of that employee's performance to draw a conclusion about his domain of work ability. Concluding that he is "slacking off" attributes underlying motives about which you probably know little. When you are uncertain, that is the time to gather more data.

New employee #2: Interviews are times of great uncertainty. It is not that your judgment is necessarily bad, but that you have not been able to judge the domain of that employee's performance from such a small sample.

The performer: The audition probably sampled too few performance attributes for you to conclude accurately about the domain of that person's ability.

The spouse: Aside from denying the possibility of a learning curve, the first few efforts constitute too small a sample to conclude accurately about the entire set of behaviors that make up the performance of the hobby.

STRAIGHT THINKING

Philosophers tell us that "logic may be regarded as the study of the most general, the most pervasive characters of both whatever is and whatever may be."[1] In general, logic is about deriving the basic truths from a set of observations or conditions. It is also about using words accurately so that they convey the exact message. Logic is also a means of gaining knowledge we do not already have by helping us figure out what follows from a given statement. Of course, the validity of what we learn from the method depends on the accuracy of the statement from which we are making the inference. Validity also depends on the rigor and precision of our logic. Aside from the "superstitious" behavior previously described, in which association is confused with causality, there are many other failures of logic common to everyday life. Noted logic author Stuart Chase once selected thirteen such fallacies, after much study and observation of what people do, nine of which are summarized in what follows:[2]

1. *Overgeneralizing.* The brain has a tendency to extract patterns from the data it receives. Sometimes you simply have to put the brakes on your brain to prevent it from "finding" a pattern too soon. Suppose you are a client of a large law firm, and you visit them one day. You walk in and see one attorney eating a candy bar. Then you see another attorney eating a candy bar. It would be a little premature to jump to the conclusions that: (a) *all* the attorneys eat candy bars, (b) all the attorneys eat *are* candy bars, or (c) the attorneys always eat candy bars when they have clients coming to visit.

2. *Give 'em an inch.* Most logic fallacies have emotional content, and strong emotions about a particular group are particularly likely to breed illogical, irrational predictions, as in: "If you let one high-school student in the drafting room this summer, you'll have to let 'em all in, and the quality of our output will suffer." Of course, there is rarely a basis for such a prediction, and it can be countered by the simple technique of asking what evidence there is to support it. If another logic fallacy is presented in lieu of real evidence, you can be sure there is nothing to the statement.

3. *Personal Attack.* First-year law students learn this: If the facts are against you, argue the law. If the law is against you, argue the facts. If the law and the facts are against you, attack your opponent. Lawyers who have a weak case can sometimes win by discrediting the opponent in a way that sidesteps the real issues. Legal eagles even have a name for this type of argument: They call it *ad hominem*, which means "to the person," to distinguish it from an *ad rem* argument, which is based on the real issue; this type of argument is also called "poisoning the well."

Suppose I have a winning case for my client, and you, the opposing attorney, get up and ask my client, "Are you now or have you ever been a member of the Communist party?" Over my objection, and despite the fact that my client's political history is irrelevant to the embezzlement charges for which he is on trial, the jury has heard something that sounds bad. The argument has nothing to do with the facts of the case being tried. It is designed solely to mislead and discredit.

4. *Superstitious Behavior*. This is the classic fallacy of logic discussed previously. It is epitomized in the wiggle dances bowlers perform, and in the belief of Chanticleer the rooster that his crowing caused the sun to rise. Just because one event follows another does not mean that there is any causal connection between them.

5. *Analogies*. If my editor were to tell me that she does not like this chapter because it does not work well with the rest of the book, I would be committing a logic fallacy to tell her, "Where would Stephen King (or any bestselling author) be if he had to cut out a chapter in each of his books?" She would no doubt reply that I am certainly not Stephen King and that I am an idiot to compare a book on brain improvement to a chilling suspense novel.

Analogies can at times be useful in illustrating a principle. The trick is not to go too far. When I compare brain fitness to muscle fitness, I mean to illustrate how mental exercise can increase the efficiency of brain function. I do not mean to suggest that the brain is "improved" in the way muscles are by exercise; neither am I using the analogy as proof that mental exercise improves the brain. On the other hand, brains and muscles can be compared rather easily along some dimensions because they both use the same "muscle proteins"—actin and myosin—for their respective functions. Thus, the analogy works well as an illustration—but only as an illustration.

Unthinking suspicions and prejudices are often provoked by analogies that compare a person's attributes or experiences with the substance of tired, old clichés. Take the phrase: "Where there's smoke, there's fire," a formulation often used to cast doubt on someone's reputation, no matter how insignificant the "smoke," or how irrelevant in present circumstances. Minds that are not prepared to think things through can easily be swayed by such expressions.

6. *What the Authorities Say*. This fallacy is characterized by people who tout credentials or charts and statistics instead of arguing the real issue. A professor who recites his credentials for answering a question hasn't answered the question; he is simply hiding his ig-

norance by telling you that all you need to know is that he is an authority.

It is quite tempting to use this fallacy in arguments. Stuart Chase relates how both the extreme Right and extreme Left champion the wisdom of Thomas Jefferson. Jefferson was in fact a facile thinker who could change his mind about issues as new facts came in. It may impress others to use Jefferson's wisdom as the acme of insight for your point of view on abortion laws, but it is not particularly relevant.

7. *Crowd Appeal.* During the Reagan administration, it became a truism to say that the president was going over the head of——— (fill in: Congress, reporters, or whoever wanted him to debate an issue) by going directly to the people. This was quite a useful tactic for "The Great Communicator," because once he had drummed up the support of the people, it became beside the point for his opponents to point out the errors in his thinking. Obviously, sometimes he was right and sometimes he was wrong, but by the force of his appeal to the crowd, he made reason irrelevant.

Of course, "the crowd" doesn't have to be everyone. Advertisers know this full well when they try to make prospective buyers become a part of an elite crowd—one of the millions of uncommon individuals buying the product. Their thinking seems to be: "After all, you certainly wouldn't want to be the only one to make a unique fashion statement, would you?" Being part of a crowd that buys these unique items to assert your own individuality is a logically contradictory notion, but it is a good way to sell merchandise.

8. *Circular Arguments.* This fallacy occurs when the thing that is being argued is offered as proof of the argument. The "proof" is often couched in highfalutin language, but it can be distilled to "The reason is because of the policy," or "We want you to do this because we want you to do this."

Joseph Heller's *Catch 22* provides a beautiful example of a circular argument interwoven as a continuing theme throughout the novel. The protagonist, a bombardier named Yossarian, wants desperately to finish his required number of bombing missions and get out of military service. But Colonel Cathcart keeps raising the number of missions the men have to fly. Yossarian pleads to Doc Daneeka to be grounded. The doctor informs him that anyone who is crazy has to be grounded; all he has to do is ask. Yossarian inquires why another man in the unit, Orr, hasn't asked to be grounded. "Because he's crazy," Daneeka tells him. The logic? "He has to be crazy to keep flying combat missions after all the close calls he's had." Moreover, when Yossarian concludes that the doctor should be able to ground Orr, he is informed that the doctor can't ground Orr because of Catch-22: Anyone who wants to get out of combat duty by asking to be grounded obviously isn't really crazy.

9. *Oversimplifying*. This is a favorite of the political-minded, whether they are running for high office or merely trying to run your office. Oversimplifiers ignore complexity and rely on slogans to obscure the issues: "Guns don't kill people. People kill people." An argument reduced to such a simple form becomes mere opinion, and it will often be supported by other logic fallacies that include overgeneralization and circular reasoning.

LOGIC IN THE BRAIN

Over the course of evolution, parts of the human brain have developed to be illogical. Actually, it is not that "illogic" was the goal but that it is helpful to the survival of the organism to make snap judgments about cause and effect based on only a single instance.

Suppose that an animal nibbles on what looks like a new supply of food and then gets sick a little while later. The animal will never touch that food again, even if the reason it got sick was because of its impending stomach virus. It does not matter to the animal that it jumped to conclusions and formed an illogical association based on that one negative event. Sometimes foods really do contain poisons. In lieu of being able to analyze the chemical content of foods, the animal is more likely to survive if it avoids foods that are associated with sickness.

Although it is tempting to pass this off as "animal behavior," scientists like Paul Rozin[3] believe that humans have evolved with the same mechanism. After all, in terms of evolutionary time, it has been only an eyeblink since humans were able to analyze the chemical content of foods. And it is likely that parts of our brains developed from the same brain circuits found to control these snap judgments about food in animals.

Our brains are capable of both logic and illogic. The form of thinking controlling our behavior is not always up to us, although we gain more control over our thoughts the more we understand how to act rationally. I once got sick at a party where I was drinking too much champagne. It just so happened that the hors d'oeuvres I was eating with the champagne were my favorite commercial crackers. By the food aversion process that normally takes place with animals, I formed a deep dislike for the "crackers that had made me sick." Never mind that I knew it was the champagne and not the crackers. The brain connection was too strong, and I avoided those crackers for two years afterward.

Cancer patients undergoing chemotherapy that makes them feel nauseous may similarly connect their nausea to foods they have eaten. It is not that they do not know better, but the powerful forces of evolution have shaped a brain that is adapted to survive by making those rash conclusions.

Although the human brain is capable of the kind of cause-and-effect illogic found in animals, it is superior to animal brains in terms of complexity. This added complexity allows for modification of the associations made from your experience. If you break a mirror and then find a $100 bill lying on the sidewalk, you would not exactly attribute your "good luck" to having broken the mirror (though some people do just the reverse with "bad luck"). However, if an animal breaks a mirror and then finds a choice piece of meat on the sidewalk, it would be more likely to break another mirror if one were available. The "cause and effect" connections are easily made in both animal and human brains, but the complexity of the human brain allows you to think through, or modify, the logic.

Through research on human brain anatomy, the fiber tracts corresponding to streams of movement, feeling, and thought have been discovered.[4] The circuits that deal with thought processes are arranged over much of the brain's volume. In fact, no single area of brain damage would rob a person of logical abilities. Parts of the brain—usually on the left side—deal with math calculation abilities, but you would have to lose most of your brain to lose all of your logic abilities.

Logic functions have something in common with memory in that they must utilize other brain functions. When logic and analysis are performed through language, language areas of the brain get a special workout. When logic and analysis have a spatial component, the spatial circuits play a part. However, it takes large areas of the brain to integrate all the analyses. Logical analysis should therefore improve if you exercise individual language and spatial functions, but logic also needs the exercise of more than individual functions. In essence, logic begets logic.

By exercising your logic functions, you can improve your abilities to reason.[5] Plato would be pleased to hear that neurophysiology has confirmed his ancient wisdom. He believed that the study of arithmetic and geometry helped to improve analytic reasoning abilities—and he was right.

Edward deBono, the noted expert on thinking, talks about two choices with regard to how you think about thinking:[6] One is that thinking is as automatic as walking or breathing. An automatic process can only be made awkward if you become conscious of it and attempt to tinker with it. The other approach is to view thinking as a skill. You may be better or worse than others at it, but you can always improve the level of your play. With the first choice, you resign yourself to your present level of existence. With the second, you take charge of your life. The techniques and exercises in the balance of this chapter will help you both to strengthen the logic of your own thinking and to identify the fallacies in other people's.

DEVELOPING AND EXERCISING THE BRAIN'S LOGIC ABILITIES

DeBono's Plus, Minus, and Interesting

This simple technique forces you to frame a decision objectively and to consider all the possible ramifications of an action. It is especially useful in preventing automatic assumptions from gaining the upper hand when you start to think about any issue. DeBono gives as an example of its effectiveness the time he asked about thirty boys (ages ten and eleven) what they thought of the idea of receiving five dollars each week just for going to school. All of them initially loved the idea and gave plenty of examples of how they would spend the money. When deBono got them to use his technique, however, they weighed all the pros and cons and decided that the latter outnumbered the former: e.g., the bigger boys would beat them up and take their money; the school would run out of money and have to raise its prices for meals or cut services; there would be quarrels about the money. In short, this method greased their logical wheels and enabled them to go beyond the easy, automatic assumption with which they began. That is why it is offered here.

SAMPLE ISSUE

The issue is "whether to judge a book by its cover." First focus your mind on the positive points. Then focus your mind on the negative points. Then think about interesting related points. A sample is provided below.

Pluses

—obtain a quicker judgment, can see more books
—provides aesthetic judgment about quality of work of publisher
—don't have to decide on basis of vague literary allusions
—helps to decide which books you really want to read
—cover art and print type is easy on the eyes

Minuses

—can't appreciate style of writing
—can't get information contained in book
—ignores substantive criticism about book
—can't get references to other books on the subject
—cover can be misleading as to content of book

Interesting

—interesting to see how publishers sell different books
—cover art can be interesting and stimulating
—interesting to see information about author
—fun to compare critics' judgments with your own
—interesting to see if cover captures spirit of book

Now it's your turn. Provide the pluses, minuses, and interesting aspects for two of the following issues.

Whether . . .

—your company should buy out a major competitor
—you should go over the head of a supervisor who is irrationally giving you a hard time
—you should move to Texas
—you should apply for a job with your company's competitor
—you should invest your bonus, windfall, or inheritance in the stock market
—you should fire an employee who has a drug problem
—you should talk to your teenage daughter about safe sex
—your aging parent should live in a nursing home

Finding Fallacies

The purpose of this exercise is to help you sensitize yourself to logic fallacies. If you don't, they can easily creep into your language, your thinking, and your actions. To begin, keep a diary of the fallacies you run across in everyday life. They can come from advertisements, speeches, written material, or conversations (your own or somebody else's). Write down the type of logic fallacy it is. Remember that statements can have more than one kind of fallacy. If you can be honest enough to record your own logic fallacies, more power to you. The more you sensitize yourself, the stronger your reasoning will become as you discipline your mind to the real issues. A brief summary of the logic fallacies discussed earlier is included below.

Summary of Logic Fallacies

Overgeneralizing—finding a "pattern" before you have enough data.

Give 'em an inch—prejudicial prediction based on scant or faulty data.

Personal Attack—avoid issue and attack opponent instead.

Superstitious Behavior—interpreting event that occurs after your behavior to be a result of that behavior.

Analogies—comparisons that make the argument look better than it is.

Appeal to Authority—presenting credentials or overloading with data to obscure or evade the issue.

Crowd Appeal—appealing to popular or emotionally positive sentiments to evade or obscure issue.

Circular Argument—using the premise of your argument as its conclusion.

Oversimplifying—distilling an argument to an extremely simple statement, as in a slogan.

CHECK YOUR PROGRESS

In each of the following statements, your job is to identify the logic fallacy. If you are having trouble, it may help if you return to the exercises in this chapter, especially the one about keeping a logic diary to further sensitize yourself to such fallacies.

Statements

A. "You shouldn't complain about having to walk a mile to school. Why, in my day, I used to walk eight miles in heavy snow to school."

B. "In the space of 176 years the Lower Mississippi has shortened itself 242 miles. This is an average of a trifle over one mile and a third per year. Therefore, any calm person, who is not blind or idiotic, can see that in the Old Silurian Period, just a million years ago next November, the River was upward of 1,300,000 miles long, and stuck out over the Gulf of Mexico like a fishing rod. And by the same token, any person can see that 742 years from now the Lower Mississippi will be only a mile and three-quarters long. . . ."
　　　　　　　　　　　　　　　　　　　　　　　　　—Mark Twain[7]

C. "Anyone who says something like that must be a (left-leaning liberal) or (right-wing fascist)."

D. "If we allow the Communists a foothold in Central America, they will soon be at our borders."

E. "Your honor, Hornswiggle is the leading authority on manure spreaders. We know he is an authority because his book on the problems of manure spreaders is the most widely used book in the field. If he weren't such an authority, his book wouldn't be so widely used."[8]

F. "If I take the vice president out to lunch, he will like my proposal."

G. "If I knowingly broke the law, I shouldn't be the governor . . . and I am the governor."

> —Statement by a governor of Arizona when
> facing criminal indictments and a recall petition

H. "An apple a day keeps the doctor away."
"You should never kill a robin because your right hand would lose all its skill."
"Bees can't sting you while you are holding your breath."
"If your right ear itches or burns, someone is saying good things about you, but if your left ear burns someone is saying bad things about you."

I. "Stock investors are courageous people."

J. From an ad in the *New Orleans Times-Picayune* about a councilman's ordinances to regulate T-shirt sales in the New Orleans French Quarter:

"The two ordinances . . . could put every legitimate business in the French Quarter out of business."

"Enacting these ordinances, in fact, would be like dropping an atomic bomb to cure a small roach problem."

"It means French Quarter, USA, becomes French Quarter, USSR."

"It means uncontrolled red tape. . . ."

"It means pushing the door wide open to political favoritism and shakedowns."

K. "I'm never going to this butcher again. After the pork chops I bought yesterday, I know the meat he sells is not fresh."

Answers

A. *Bad analogy* (faulty comparison), with a hint of *personal attack*. Times have changed, and it is possible that the real issue has to do with other factors—medical problems, desire to have time for extracurricular activities, etc. The old-timer's argument is an attempt to seal the discussion by changing the issue. The suggestion that the child is unworthy because of a lack of fortitude has the markings of a personal attack, in which an attempt is made to make the opponent the issue.

B. If this were not so obviously a satire, the logic faults would include an *appeal to (statistical) authority* and *oversimplification* of the data. When someone makes an extrapolation from a limited set of data, it is smart to examine the hidden premises. In Mark Twain's statement, the premise that the rate of shortening of the river has always been and will always be the same is never brought forth. If Twain were serious, he would be hoping you would not catch his oversimplification of the data.

C. This is a standard *personal attack* in which the aim is to distract from the real issue by casting aspersions on the opponent.

D. This *"give 'em an inch"* argument is designed to prejudice the listeners against the target. There may be evidence for expansionist tendencies, but the situation is far too complex to make a statement such as that. The argument, therefore, includes an *oversimplification*.

E. This is classic *circular reasoning*. No evidence other than a book which is said to be widely used is given for Farnsworth's authority. We know he is an authority because his book is widely used, and anyone who writes a widely used book must be an authority. The conclusion is used as a premise.

F. Assuming the vice president will be deciding the value of your proposal solely on the basis of its merits, this statement is probably a case of *superstitious behavior*. The speaker has perhaps seen the vice president deciding favorably on a proposal after going out to lunch with its author. However, if the vice president can in fact be influenced by such a simple gesture as being taken out to lunch, then the statement reflects a real causal connection between the behavior and the outcome, and there is no fallacy.

G. The governor committed a *circular logic* fallacy. He asserts that he should not be governor if he knowingly broke the law. Since he is the governor, he could not have knowingly broken the law. His statement thus evades the issue of whether independent evidence of his behavior exists.

H. All these statements are characteristic of *superstitious behavior*. There may or may not be evidence to support any of them, but the point is that the beliefs were probably established through a quick association between behavior and a positive outcome. The person who associated holding one's breath with preventing a bee sting, for example, probably had this happen at least once, but that experience does not constitute proof for the rule. Folk wisdom is sometimes proven true, but not by anecdotal evidence of this kind.

I. This is an *overgeneralization*; all the stock investors *you know* may be courageous, but it is a sure bet you do not know all the stock investors in the world. If you were to engage in scientific sampling techniques, you have a chance of making this statement with accuracy. However, if you simply are finding a "pattern" on the basis of the first "data" you run across, you are overgeneralizing.

J. Several logic fallacies are contained in these statements, which are characteristic of political advertising. First, the *emotional appeal* is evident: Few people could like the idea of an ordinance that would lead to "political favoritism" or "shakedowns." A *false analogy* is apparent in the comparison with dropping an atomic bomb to snuff out a roach problem. The comparison certainly brings forth a strong image, but the image has little to do with the characteristics of the problem. Another *false analogy* is presented in the comparison with USSR bureaucratic control. *Oversimplifying* is also evident in the distillation of the complex issue to the sloganistic wording of an ad.

K. *Oversimplification via statistical reasoning.* Unfortunately for the butcher, most people would not care that the "sample" was too small, especially if it was their first time at the shop. A larger sample is needed to draw a conclusion about all the meat at this shop.

A FEW MORE LOGIC TWISTERS[9]
Acrobats

Most acrobats are smart. All acrobats are physically fit. Therefore:

A. Smart acrobats are also physically fit.
B. Brain power and fitness don't go well together.
C. All acrobats who are physically fit are smart.
D. Most acrobats are smart about physical fitness.

Answer

A. Both smart and not-so-smart acrobats (i.e., *all* acrobats) are physically fit.

Spellers

Statistics indicate that men misspell more words than women. It may be concluded that:

A. Men who cast aspersions on women's spelling abilities are wrong.
B. Men are actually better spellers but write more frequently.
C. Men and women spell equally well but men don't like to use spelling checkers.
D. Most technical writers are men.
E. There is not enough information to justify any one of these conclusions.

Answer

E. If you got this wrong, you should remind yourself to test your conclusions tightly against the data. Preconceived notions often get confused with logical conclusions.

Fast Checks

Shelley, Sally, Susan, and Samantha are fast check writers. Samantha is faster than Susan but Sally is faster than Samantha. Susan is faster than Shelley but Sally is faster than Susan. Therefore:

A. Both Shelley and Sally are faster than Samantha.
B. Samantha is faster than Shelley but is slower than Susan.
C. Samantha is even faster than Shelley than she is faster than Susan.
D. None of the above.

Answer

C. It is helpful to draw up a speed scale and place each check writer's relative speed on the scale. The order from faster to slower is Sally, Samantha, Susan, Shelley. From here, the logic work is almost complete.

Logic Problems

When you are asked to find the fallacies in someone else's thinking, you are using some of your own logic abilities, but not calling on all your resources. However, when you are asked to reason out a logical solution to a problem, you force your brain to utilize more of its skills. You will find that working through the following problems will help you discipline your reasoning abilities and attain a higher level of mental performance in all areas of life.[10]

Keep in mind that "disciplining your reasoning abilities" is tantamount to exercising the brain circuits that control logic. As these cells are exercised, they adapt to the increased activity. It is this adaptation that provides the positive change in your logic abilities —just as any form of practice improves performance.

Logic Problem #1: Strange Potato Chips, Inc. has now developed potato chips decorated with colors and geometric shapes. You are given four potato chips as shown below. Each one is either blue or yellow on one side and has either a triangle or square on the other side. In what order must you pick up and turn over the potato chips to have enough information in the fewest potato chips possible to answer the question: Does every blue potato chip have a square printed on its other side?

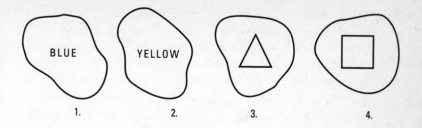

1.   2.   3.   4.

Answer: First, #2 is out, because you are only concerned with blue potato chips. Similarly, you are not immediately concerned with #4: If it is yellow on the back, you cannot answer your question. If it is blue, you still cannot know whether the rule is true for all blue potato chips. It is best to start with #1: If it does not have a square on back, you have answered the question. If it does have a square on back, you cannot prove the rule and will need to turn over another potato chip. Turn over potato chip #3: If it is blue on back, the answer to the question is no. If it is yellow on back, the answer is yes. This is because all blue potato chips will have a square on back no matter what color #4 has. The solution involves first #1 and then #3.

Logic Problem #2: A bookshop receives three boxes labeled "Old Books," "New Books," and "Old and New Books." However, the labels are all misplaced. By selecting only one book from one box—without feeling around or peeking—how can the bookseller label each box correctly?

Answer: Select one book from the box labeled "Old and New Books." If the book is old, then that box is now labeled "Old Books" and the remaining two boxes are to be labeled "New Books" and "Old and New Books." Since you know that the box previously labeled "New Books" cannot have only new books if it is mislabeled, then it is the "Old and New Books" box, and the third box is labeled "New Books."

Logic Problem #3: Three equally qualified women apply for a job. Since the prospective employer cannot differentiate on the basis of their backgrounds, she decides to try a little test. The job will go to the first applicant who solves the problem. The employer places a red or green mark on each applicant's forehead. The three are told that each has a red or green mark, and each is to raise her hand if she sees a red mark on the forehead of either of the other two. The first one to tell (logically) what color she has will get the job. Each woman raised her hand, and after a few seconds one woman came up with the answer. What color was her mark, and how did she figure it out? (Hint: Your logic will have to extend beyond the placement of colored marks.)

Answer: First, there cannot be two or three green marks; otherwise, not every applicant could have raised her hand. There must be two or three red marks, but how did the winner know what her mark was? This is where the logic has to extend beyond the colored marks. The winner has to reason about what the other two could know. The winner realizes that the two losers see either one red and one green or two reds. If either of the losers had seen one red and one green, then she would have known her mark to be red, and she would not have lost. Obviously, each of the losers saw two reds, so the winner's mark must have been red.

Variations on Raymond Smullyan Logic Puzzles

Logic Problem #4: Here is a variant on a Raymond Smullyan puzzle: Judy, one of triplets named Judy, Ellen, and Susan, has the keys to the city. Judy and Ellen never tell the truth, but Susan always tells the truth. The trouble is, you can't tell them apart. When you meet this triplet, you want to know whether she is Judy. The city charter says you are allowed to ask her only one question that can be answered yes or no, but the question cannot have more than three words. What is the question?

Answer: "Are you Ellen?" Ellen will lie and say no. Susan will tell the truth and say no. Judy is the only one who will say yes.

Logic Problem #5: Here's another Smullyan variant: The rule of the hair salon is that if any hair cutter cuts a cutter's hair—whether her own or another cutter's—then all cutters have to cut her hair (though not all at the same time). Sally, Sue, Sheila, and Sara are all hair cutters in the salon. Sally has cut Sue's hair. Has Sara cut Sheila's hair?

Answer: Yes. If anyone has cut anyone's hair, they all have cut hair and have had their hair cut.

Logic Problem #6: You meet somebody from Truth or Lies at a cocktail party. But there's a twist: All truth tellers are accurate, and all liars are inaccurate. If you ask someone from Truth whether one plus one equals two, the person will tell you yes, because she is accurate and tells the truth. But if you ask the same question of a person from Lies, she will also say yes. This is because she doesn't think one plus one equals two—she is inaccurate in her judgment. So what one question do you ask to find where she is from?

Answer: Ask: "Are you the accurate truthteller?" The truthteller will be correct and honest in telling you yes, and the liar—who believes herself (incorrectly) to be accurate and honest—will say no.

Logic Problem #7: You come to a fork in the road. One path leads to the town of Truth in which everyone tells the truth. The other path leads to the town of Lies in which no one tells the truth. A resident of one of the towns sits at the fork in the road. By asking one question, how could you determine which path leads to Truth?

Answer: Ask: "Which is the path to your town?" Both the truth teller and the liar will point out the correct path.

Logic Problem #8: Two children are boasting about the speed of their bicycles. But it is a reverse boasting—they each believe they have the slower bike. They are aware that if they try to race, each might go a little slower than his bike is capable of just to prove the point. They come to you for advice. In two words, you can tell them how to decide the issue. What do you say?

Answer: "Switch bikes." Then each child will be motivated to have his friend's bike go faster to prove his own the slower.

Logic Problem #9: The Murder-Suspect Cases. These are a take-off from Dr. Arenberg's logic problems, which are used in neuropsychological assessment. Your job is to figure out the murderer from the information given. In each case, the murderer kills whenever he or she is present. A sample is explained below.

People Present In the House:	What Happened to the Victims:
Case #1 Butler, Maid, Gardener	Died
Butler, Uncle, Gardener	Died
Butler, Maid, Guest	Lived

Answer: The gardener did it.

In this case, the murderer must be the gardener, since he was present when the victims died *and* absent when the victims lived. None of the other suspects have this logical pattern.

Case #2 Butler, Maid, Brother	Died
Gardener, Maid, Brother	Died
Butler, Maid, Sister	Died

Answer: The maid did it.

Case #3 Guest, Aunt, Maid	Died
Guest, Aunt, Butler	Lived

Answer: The maid did it.

Case #4   Brother, Father, Uncle .... Died
Brother, Father, Aunt .... Died
Brother, Father, Cousin .... Died
Gardener, Father, Uncle .... Died

Answer: The father did it.

Case #5   Uncle, Butler, Maid .... Died
Uncle, Butler, Mother .... Died
Uncle, Guest, Maid .... Died

Answer: The uncle did it.

Case #6   Aunt, Uncle, Sister .... Lived
Maid, Butler, Sister .... Lived
Aunt, Butler, Mother .... Lived
Aunt, Spouse, Sister .... Lived
Maid, Uncle, Guest .... Lived

Answer: If there are no victims, there are no murderers.

As You Become More Analytical

As your logic abilities improve, you may notice that you are taking someone else's word as evidence for or against an issue less and less. This is because you are analyzing those words for logic content and logic fallacies. The following recommendations, adapted from Robert Gula's book *Nonsense and How to Overcome It*, can help you check the progress of your logic abilities. Try to sense how far along you are by how easy it is to notice . . .

—whether people are speaking in absolutes. Words like *all*, *none*, *no one*, *never*, and *always* are tip-offs.
—whether generalizations that are unsupported or supported from only one or two examples are used
—if emotional language is used to sway opinion
—the difference between opinion and evidence
—whether the evidence is directed to the topic or to some related issue
—whether the conclusions of an argument follow logically from the premises
—whether the evidence is complete or excludes unfavorable or unsupportive data

A Not-So-Horrifying Scenario

If you have gotten this far, I will assume that you are examining the
things people say more closely. Statements that you might previously
have let pass are now being processed by a more analytical brain.
The fallacies in statements about which you might have felt a vague
unease (without understanding why) can now be unmasked. You are
not so easily manipulated by subtle twists of language.

As another means of checking your progress, put yourself in
the following scenario and observe your ability to remain emotionally
detached in order to be alert to the attempts to damage your well-
being:

> You are working late the day after you submitted the new
> marketing proposal to the vice president. He storms into your
> office without knocking, and is he angry about the proposal.
> "Well, you've done it this time."
> "How's that?"
> "This is the worst piece of trash I have ever seen. I don't even
> know why I'm talking to you about it. I ought to fire you for
> submitting something this bad."
> "What's bad about it?"
> "You've gone way overboard on your budget. Even you should
> know that with a budget that big, we'll never break even with the
> product. You're an idiot to think that the concept is any good—
> no one likes it. It treats the consumers as if they were ants. Our
> company has a long tradition of treating our buyers better than
> that. What do you want to do, wreck the company you work for?
> Are you that callous to our needs?"

How you choose to respond to this attack depends on a number
of factors: Whether your antagonist blows hot and cold, whether he
listens to reason, the nature and duration of your relationship to
him, to the company, etc. However, by now, it is probably an easy
matter for you to pick out the errors in your antagonist's logic. Any
of the logical issues involved in the assumptions about how you treat
the buyers, whether you are callous, or why you wanted to spend
the money that particular way are fair game. Although it is sometimes

difficult to withstand such an attack, you will be better able to prevent yourself from getting distracted by the emotional components, better able to focus on the real issues under discussion and to identify the deviations from it, as you exercise your analytic abilities. You will develop a "sense" for logic, complete with an ability to use it to your advantage.

EFFECTIVE problem solving in the real world requires a combination of memory, logic, and insight. As we add memories of our experiences with space, language, and logic, our brains acquire even better discipline and rigor. But can we also enhance our creativity? Can we develop that "sideways logic" that is such an important aid in solving some problems? The next chapter, on creativity, shows how we can focus our brain exercises so that we become more receptive to new ideas and better able to initiate them ourselves.

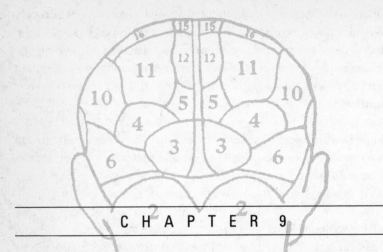

CHAPTER 9

Creating a Creative Brain

Cartoonists often portray a character's brilliant idea as a light bulb turning on inside her "thought cloud," thus tacitly acknowledging the brilliance of Edison's discovery. Yet revolutionary discoveries—ones that transform our ways of looking at the world—come about in many different ways. Sometimes they do simply pop into the head, full-blown and ready to be used without much retooling. More often, for example with Edison and his light bulb, the final shape or feel of the idea is known, but a great deal of practical maneuvering is required to realize the final product. Whichever way the final idea is formed, it is certain that the mind —consciously or subconsciously—must sift through its store of raw information.[1]

Heuristics are devices that aid in thinking. Through his observations of how people solve problems creatively, noted psychologist Howard Gardner has come up with a list of the methods (heuristics) people use when they are being especially creative.[2] His list is adapted and summarized below. Although no one can assert that a creative genius consciously uses any of these heuristics, it is evident that they can be used to one's creative advantage at times when the correct solution to a problem does not suddenly appear. If some of these devices appear contradictory, it should be kept in mind that problems differ in their domains as well as the starting point of their solutions.

CREATIVITY FINDERS

1. *Generalize the Issue:* Push your thinking upward from the set of elements you are working on to a higher (larger) realm of elements which contains the problem. The morale problem you are having with a few employees may only reflect difficulties they are having in their personal lives, but it could also indicate a problem with the way their working lives are structured, or even a "higher level" problem with the nature of the rules under which all work in your organization is governed.

2. *Specialize the Issue:* Push your thinking down to a realm of greater detail about the problem. My professor in a creative writing class once told a fellow student that it was easy to write a story about anything. You just need to look out your window. "But how?" the student protested. "All I see is the same old thing—the same cars, the same houses, the same people. Everything is old hat." The professor assured him that he could do it if only he paid greater attention to detail. "First, do you see the house on the corner, the one with the red door? The door is sturdy, solid. It has a brass knocker, and there's writing on the strike plate. The door has a fisheye peephole, the kind that amasses a large part of the nearby world into a concentrated view. A large welcome mat sits in front of the house. It is always clean. Every morning at ten o'clock sharp, an old woman emerges from the house. She has a limp. She has neatly combed white hair. She often paints her lips with bright orange lipstick. She sits on the porch swing to greet the mailman and anyone walking

close to the house with a dog, but she won't talk to a mother with her child." The student was amazed at the story he finally saw in a scene which had not interested him at all. "That's nothing," the professor said. "I haven't even described her neighbor."

3. *Ferret Out Analogies:* Try to find a problem or situation that can be usefully compared or contrasted to the present one. Lawyers do this all the time when they cannot find a good precedent but instead find an old case involving problems similar to those presented by the case under discussion, the outcome of which they would like to see applied to the current case. Analogies, no matter how persuasive their similarities, should not be confused with logic (see the preceding chapter for clarification of the difference between the two), but they can be very helpful when creativity as opposed to logic is required. You can't reason your way to the solving of certain problems, but you *can* sometimes get there with an analogy.

4. *Find Smaller Modules:* Try to find a simpler problem within the larger one, and then build on that solution to solve the larger problem. If your child is having difficulty with a school science project, you might help him break the overall project down into its modules—rationale, comparisons, observations, conclusions, et cetera. Similarly, suppose you are having trouble devising a new marketing concept. A "smaller module" to which you might apply yourself is the product or logo design. A success with this smaller problem can often transfer to the larger one.

5. *Propose a Possible Solution and Work Backward:* This method assumes that you know something about the realm of possible solutions, and that you know how to think logically, while still retaining mental flexibility. Mental flexibility is a trait that allows you to come up with multiple solutions, instead of getting fixated on one. For example, suppose someone has been rearranging files in your office. You want to know who, and why this person has entered your office without asking. Further suppose that the rearranging is systematic and concerned with a particular class of files. This knowledge establishes the domain of possible solutions. Now, try fitting your supervisor into the solution slot and see if he fits. If, when you work backward, you find that he would not have been concerned with *those* files, you have eliminated one possible solution. Knowing

you will have to fit other possible culprits into the solution slot induces you to keep your mind open to all the potential solutions.

6. *Describe the Characteristics a Solution Should Have, and Then Try to Attain Each of Them:* This method is related to the previous one in that it requires some prior knowledge about the solution. But you do not have to know what the solutions are to know what features of them you want to attain. Suppose you want to invent a better mousetrap—say, one that doesn't harm the mouse in any way. Before you can actually solve this problem, you should know the features of the mousetraps which you are trying to improve. Then you might list some of the features of the yet-to-be-determined solution: size, bait, sticky substance on bottom of trap (one solution), structure of the trap door (another solution), et cetera.

Finding the Child Within

In many ways creativity is completely unlike analytical or logical thought. The kinds of thought evaluated on intelligence tests can be useful in solving certain problems, but they are not always helpful in the creation of new ideas, metaphors, or modes of thought. Before logical and analytical thinking sets in, young children are relatively free of the modes of thought that restrict the creation of ideas. Serious artists often recognize that the bonds of adulthood must be broken. Picasso once said, "I used to draw like Raphael, but it has taken a whole lifetime to learn how to draw like a child."

The exercises in this chapter are designed to bring out the child in you. Unlike in the previous chapter, when you had to use "adult reasoning," you will now be called upon to forget logic. The idea is not to analyze or think through solutions in a stepwise manner, but to let your mind flow and wander around various possibilities. Be encouraged to forget the adult norms and attack each exercise with a child's simplicity. Remember that no one is watching, except the child inside.

Creativity in the Brain

You can be creative in the exercise of any of your brain functions; you can achieve new representations of the spatial world, as a visual artist does. You can make up new tunes and rhythms, and if you learn the language of music you can record your ideas as a composer does. If you are athletic, you can achieve new ways of moving your body. With language, you are creative every time you use a metaphor that brings together disparate images that work well when joined. You are also being creative with language every time you make a joke or formulate a pun.

Creativity is not a matter of any one special ability. Rather, it involves the ability to be flexible in the exercise of several (or more) of your brain's functions. It is the difference between *convergent thinking*, with its search for one true solution, and *divergent thinking*, in which the brain freely ranges over possible solutions to a problem. The different functions within a creative mind work together, exchanging data and building momentum in a synergistic fashion. The Russian memory expert who was able to remember a complex mathematical nonsense formula was not just accomplished in memory. If you recall, he reinforced his natural mnemonic gifts through the use of his language function, which enabled him to invent a story incorporating all the elements of the formula. His capacity for a synergistic combining of brain functions also expressed itself through sensory mixes, in which one type of sensation—for example, sound—evoked another—color or touch. This flexibility is the epitome of creativity.

Because of the complexity of our brains, most people have the potential for creativity. By contrast, simple organisms with relatively simple nervous systems tend to exhibit more stereotypic, inflexible behavior.

It is easy to see how complexity leads to flexibility if you consider computer programs. Once, I developed a graph-drafting program for my students. To make the program comprehensive but easy to use, I developed the various graphing functions—which can be thought of as brain functions—in program modules. Then I fit each modular function into the master program in a hierarchy. To make them all work, I then had to make connections between the modules: The module that handled the placement of points or lines on the graph had to "talk" to the module that analyzed those points, and the module that determined the color of the points and lines had to "talk" to all the other modules.

After fitting in each module, I tested the master program to see how everything worked together. I began to notice something as the number of modules—the complexity—grew. The program began to take on flexible characteristics that I had never intended. For example, the language module allowed the user to erase all the lines on the graph while retaining all the math information loaded in the math module. You could then put an analysis on the screen without having the points showing.

The complexity of the program wasn't even in the same order of magnitude as that of your brain, but it did show a rudimentary creativity—the ability to achieve a goal through a sideways, flexible logic.

What is so exciting about your brain is that it is built in a similar way with modules arranged in a communicative hierarchy. For example, each feature-analyzer module "sees" one part of the visual world. That part may be an upright edge, a slanted edge, or a slanted edge moving in one direction. Higher in the hierarchy, the modules join to take care of visual scenes in each eye. As the hierarchy builds further, the brain is able to put together the pattern from both eyes that we call visual perception. We are able to see things as whole objects, not as collections of pieces of vision.

The analyzers that enable you to decode the visual world are built to communicate not only with each other but with other parts of the brain. The visual area of the brain communicates with memory and auditory areas. You are able to close your eyes and "hear" the concert from memory as well as "see" the performers on the stage. This flexibility is in itself a creative act. You can also imagine the appearance of things you cannot see because you can rotate visual images in your mind's eye. When you are using language, either writing or talking, you can include visual images that evoke similar images in the reader or listener. The communication between visual modules and other brain functions allows you to insert novel visual images into your other functions. In essence, this complex interplay of communications means that your brain is built to be creative.

The major difference between brain systems and computer software is in the complexity of the brain. The brain is more flexible because it is many orders of magnitude more complex. Activating the transfer of information among the brain's many functions will stimulate this flexibility, giving you greater creativity not only in problem solving and other practical abilities but in a general appreciation of and response to life.

The Left and the Right of It

Nobel laureate Roger Sperry once observed that "Each [brain] hemisphere . . . has its own . . . private sensations, perceptions, thoughts, and ideas all of which are cut off from the corresponding experiences in the opposite hemisphere."[3] Sperry had been monitoring patients who underwent split-brain surgery for epilepsy. The aim of this surgery is to cut the broad band of fibers that communicate between the brain hemispheres and allow epileptic storms to spread. Since these nerve fibers normally let your right and left brains "talk" to one another, the patients end up with brain halves that function separately.

When Sperry tested these patients, he found that right brains tend to think about the appearance of objects, while left brains think about function. For example, when you see a pair of open scissors, your right brain is likely to register its openness and crisscrossing appearance, while your left brain thinks about its ability and readiness to cut something.

This discovery left a lot of people wondering whether all brain functions are divided into right and left brain modes of activity. Moreover, if all our activities are of two basic types, maybe our brains are made of two basic components. Historically, we have tended to divide the intellect into two types. The types are extrapolations of what we know about the characteristics of left and right hemispheres in information processing. One type, corresponding to left hemisphere functioning, is logical, analytical, rational, sequential, and verbal. The other, the right hemisphere function, is intuitive, non-verbal, spatial, simultaneous, synthetic, and analogical.[4]

We have probably gone too far in assigning these higher-order abilities to exclusively right or left hemisphere modes of activity. For example, how could we possibly test for or assign a physical location to a "synthetic" function? Moreover, even if the hemispheres do tend to specialize, the distinctions between them are blurred because normal brains have millions of fibers connecting the two hemispheres and enabling them to communicate with and be affected by each other. Whatever different tendencies our two brain hemispheres have are communicated thoroughly between the two sides. For these reasons, when we talk about enhancing creativity, it is more important to facilitate brain flexibility and communication than to concentrate on cocktail party dichotomies.

BENEFITS OF ENHANCED CREATIVITY

This section can itself be made into an exercise in creativity. The exercise is simple: To think of all the possible reasons you might benefit from enhanced creativity. (You may add your own ideas whenever you feel like it.)

—Have more fluidity in thought; not get stuck when trying to solve problems.
—Be more relaxed and less anxious when you need to solve a problem.
—Increase your confidence in ideas.
—Waste less time because you can get more done.
—Increase your enjoyment in solving problems.
—Become more understanding of and empathetic to the ideas of others.
—Learn to be able to discard habitual thought pattterns.

Being creative entails all these things. People who are being creative often get lost in the activity, and sometimes lose awareness of the outside world. They achieve "flow states" (see chapter 4), in which their minds are joined with the activity in a rush of enjoyable creative output.

Creativity changes your attitude about change. Life is always changing, and it is not enough to react passively to change. With liberated creativity and imagination, you do not have to be *dragged along* by these changes. You can become one of the forces behind the ever-changing world. By enhancing your creativity, you can make your own future, or at least be prepared to make effective use of what you find in your future.

EXERCISING CREATIVITY

Creativity involves an ability to leap off the tracks of thought. If you've ever said to yourself that you're not creative, you are cheating yourself of powers that every human possesses. Although some people are a little uncomfortable not having the answers to problems stored and readily available in memory, others like the search for the solution. It can be pleasurable to run your thoughts along byways that have not been used frequently, and it can be a real treat to find an elegant solution for a problem.

To be creative, your thought only has to be new to you; it does not have to be the first. That is why it is so easy to exercise your creative powers. You do not have to learn things and store them in memory. You only need to stimulate the movement of your mind around to different ideas. As you perform these exercises, try to feel your mind loosening up as your habitual patterns of thought begin to break up and change.[5]

SPATIAL CREATIVITY
Ink Blots

Hermann Rorschach devised an inkblot method (the Rorschach test) that many psychologists still use as a projective test to illuminate thoughts and emotions. The idea is to stare at a meaningless shape and let your mind provide form, content, structure, or meaning by projecting your inner wishes, feelings, or ideas onto the shape.

Opposite are two inkblots. You may view each of them from whatever orientation or position you prefer. For each, let your mind flow around and through the shapes. Take your time to allow your mind to change. Give a detailed description of what you see in each inkblot. It can be a whole scene, as if taken from a movie. Or it can be like a photograph or a single object. The description can be of something you know, or it can come completely out of your imagination. After you have the details in mind, write them down. Then do it all over again for each inkblot, deriving completely new descriptions the second time. This is when your creativity really begins to flow—when you alter your perceptions of an image you put together out of your own creativity.

Creating an Image

Two sets of lines and shapes are provided below. Complete the drawing of an image from each by using the lines and shapes as a logical part of the image. You do not have to be able to draw, but try to be clever, original, and detailed. You may turn the shapes in any orientation you want to achieve your image.

 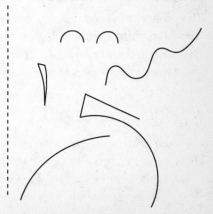

Alternatives

The following drawing does not represent anything in particular. The idea is to increase your ability to shift from pattern to pattern. Your job is to list several things it could represent. Make your list before you look at mine, then add to mine if you like. When you get through, try this exercise on your own simple nonsense drawing.

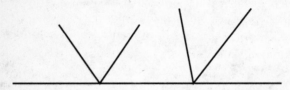

My List of Representations

—a flea's eye view of a dog's back
—two cockroaches crawling up on the side of a table as seen from across the table
—microscopic view of two pencils poised for writing
—the points of two missiles about to pierce the ground
—four spears thrown from opposite sides into the ground landing in two places
—antennae from two old televisions
—top view of two Martians sticking their feelers out of a window

LOGICAL AND ANALYTICAL CREATIVITY

The concept behind this section seems to be a contradiction; creativity is usually freer than analytic thought. However, you can get into an analytic rut when you are trying to solve a problem. One of the best ways to get out is to free your mind's creative powers.

Logic Alternatives

This exercise is similar to the spatial creativity exercise you just did. It is especially easy to perform while you are commuting to and from work, but you can do it anywhere at anytime. It is designed to get you to be flexible with logical possibilities. Please notice that it is not a substitute for hard analytic thought but simply a flexibility exercise.

> You start with a concrete image of a scene—somebody doing something that is at least a little out of the ordinary. It could be somebody consciously running a red light after first stopping at the intersection, it could be your secretary blowing up balloons when you walk in in the morning. Whatever your scene, quickly do a mental scan of all the logical possibilities. They can be fantastic or ordinary, but the only requirement is that they fit as an "explanation" of the scene. A sample follows below.

> Scene: Man running red light after stopping at intersection.

SAMPLE EXPLANATIONS
—He forgot his lunch and is racing home to get it.
—He is neurotic and always does this as his private means of flouting the law, but he has to check first to make sure the law is not around.
—He is being chased but fears hitting someone in the cross traffic.
—He was going to rush his wife to the hospital to have their baby, and in his hurry he left her at the house and is going back home to get her, but he is afraid of hitting someone in the cross traffic.
—He has had a mental lapse and automatically hit the gas pedal when he saw the green turning arrow come on.

What Would Happen If . . .
Here is an oldie but a goodie. You simply list all the logical implications of a given proposition. For example, what would happen if . . .

> . . . the moon were made of green cheese.

> —We could send astronauts to mine it and provide the earth with a readily available source of food.

—Different poetry or song lyrics would be developed about the moon.

—Advertisers would have a new concept.

—Space stations on the moon would have to import less food.

—Dairy farmers would lose a significant market and might complain.

Now it is your turn. What would happen if . . .

. . . you switched places with your immediate superior or subordinate for one year.

. . . your immediate superior or subordinate had eyes in the back of her head.

. . . your company were to be bought out by a competitor.

. . . you couldn't drive a car for the next six months.

. . . you and your best friend switched lives for a month.

. . . you knew when you were going to die.

Plot a Murder Mystery

Now that you have some practice in developing logical alternatives, I would like to add structure to the flexibility exercise. You are going to create a murder mystery plot. It is actually quite easy once you get the hang of it, and can be wonderfully absorbing and enjoyable. The importance of the exercise lies in getting you to channel your creative flow to make the logic work. Instead of creating individual "explanations" for an event, each with its own internal logic, you will be creating explanations for a murder scene that fit an overall logic. Once you get the hang of this, you may find it's something you can do to fill up the time you spend commuting, or standing in line at the bank, or waiting to see the dentist. You might even have to caution yourself against falling into your fantasy life so much that you miss your stops or begin to emit strange chuckles.

Start with an image of the murder scene and include the murder weapon. You might then think of whose fingerprints are on it and whether they belong to the murderer or someone who handled the device before the gloved murderer used it. There is, of course, a body. You should think of the relationship of the dead person to a loved one and whether they had a quarrel before the death. Then think of two or three people connected with the dead person or loved one and their relationships to the murder. Once you have your basic characters and the murder in mind, provide a set of "explanations" for the events of the murder scene. My example follows below.

Scene: Well-known mystery writer is found dead at his word processor by a fan whom he had arranged to meet at his house. It was obvious that death had been caused by the word processor blowing up when the writer turned it on. His spouse had been out shopping. Fan's wife is in love with the picture of the writer on the bookjacket and has been talking about him for two weeks. Writer had met fan's wife's sister and enjoyed a brief fling with her a year ago.

SAMPLE PLOT EXPLANATIONS

—Spouse is the murderer because she is the only one who could have known her husband is away from his word processor long enough for her to wire it.
—Spouse is the murderer because she has a degree in electronics and knows how to wire the word processor with explosives.
—Fan is not the murderer because he is a lover of mystery novels, particularly the novels of the deceased.
—Fan is not the murderer because he was expecting to get a hint of the writer's next book at their meeting.
—Fan's wife is not the murderer because she knows the writer only through his book jacket photo and is in love with that image.
—Fan's wife's sister is not the murderer because she broke off the affair for another man who had a real job.
—Death was not suicide because the writer has devoted and adoring fans.

There. You do not have to construct a particularly good plot to reap the benefits of this exercise and there are no right or wrong "explanations." The point is to get your imagination flowing within the constraints of a plot scenario that has its own internal logic. If you want to take the time to add more characters and fill out the scenario with a greater amount of detail about motivation, opportunity, temperament of the protagonists, etc., you could be on your way to writing your first mystery novel.

Creative Language Exercises

Limerick Sense

Because of their short and simple structure, limericks are easy to create. The rhymes force you to use language in a certain way, but the constraints of rhyme and rhythm are the only ones you have to observe. Writing limericks is an exercise in creative flexibility through the medium of words, which means that your language function is getting a simultaneous workout. One important point: Try timing yourself as a measure of your flexibility. See if your speed increases as your language creativity improves. As with most brain exercises, this is an effective way to monitor your progress. A couple of sample limericks are offered below. You could start by writing a second stanza for each, or make up your own from scratch.

> A sailor with Vasco da Gama
> Set to mend his llama pajama
> Old Vasco replied
> If that's land we spied
> You can hunt for the right kind of llama

> A clock that runs counterclockwise
> Gives me lows when it should give me highs
> I feel it is three
> When it's nine that I see
> And I really should be closing my eyes

Word Sense

This one was developed by Lewis Carroll, author of *Alice in Wonderland*. It is useful for flexibility with words. You simply change one letter at a time in the first word until you end up with the finished word. The trick is that each change has to produce a new word. Try to make the transformations in as few words as possible. When you finish with these, create your own.

WARM to COLD: WARM WARD CARD CORD COLD
DULL to MIND:
SMART to THINK:

Punning and Humor

Thought expert Edward deBono talks about lateral thinking as a process of switching patterns within a patterned system. This translates as the ability to look at "familiar" things in different ways. There are quotations around "familiar," because you could be looking at new things in your old way as well as recognizing old things you have seen many times.

With language, punning and humor provide perfect examples of lateral thinking—escaping from one pattern of thought into another. The habitual way of hearing a word or understanding a meaning takes on a new form when the pun or joke is heard. But hearing a pun or understanding a joke are only passive means of experiencing language creativity. The purpose of this exercise is to get you to flex your own language creativity muscles.

PUNNING[6]

Think of other words or word patterns these target words sound like, and provide a pun for each. Then write down the pun definition as I have done for the first three words. If you want more creativity in these exercises, try making up for one or more words a little story in which the punch line is the pun.

Illegal—A sick eagle.
Dumbbell—A bell that is not too bright.
Island—Land mass shaped like an eye when viewed from above.
Ragamuffin—
Kaleidoscope—
Specialize—

Tomahawk—
Brocade—
Bankroll—
Holy water—

MORE PUNNING

A game many of us played as kids was to make up titles of books written by a punned author. The classic in this genre is *Yellow River* by I. P. Freely. A few examples are provided, but the exercise is to provide five more of your own.

Going on the Wagon by Al Cohol
Stretching Exercises by I. M. Lissome
Music on the Water by Viola Lake

Pure Creative Exercise—Daydreaming

Many important discoveries in art and science have come about through dreaming or daydreaming. The chemist Friedrich August von Kekule discovered one of the most important facts about modern chemistry—ring structures—through a daydream.[7] Many of Mozart's symphonies originated in daydreams, as well as Nietzsche's *Thus Spake Zarathustra*. As Arthur Koestler says in his important book on creativity, *The Act of Creation*, "the temporary relinquishing of conscious controls liberates the mind from certain constraints which are necessary to maintain the disciplined routines of thoughts but may become an impediment to the creative leap. . . ."

Daydreaming may be a natural way to use brain power efficiently. Daydreams help us relax and focus, and there is some evidence that people who daydream more than average (but not to excess) have above average psychological strengths.

These exercises are designed simply to encourage your ability to daydream, to release you from the normal disciplined modes of thought. You can daydream anytime—while ironing or commuting or during a brief break from work. Because daydreaming has not had such a glorious history—it has often been associated with laziness—some of you may be a little rusty. However, once you achieve flexibility with your daydreams, you can apply them to problems that seem unsolvable no matter how hard you have pushed with disciplined thinking.

And don't be discouraged by the Walter Mitty flavor of your daydreams. For one thing, your daydreams are private. No one has access to them unless you want them to. Be encouraged to daydream about images related to your job, position, or people you normally deal with. If you want to fantasize about becoming someone totally unrelated to who you are, it will certainly do you no harm.

> Daydream #1: Imagine yourself at work on one of the difficult problems you face in your job. The problem suddenly melts, and you achieve the breakthrough. You rush into the managers' meeting to announce your solution, and they give you applause, something that has never happened in the company's history. Your solution creates an enormous amount of business in important new markets.

> Daydream #2: Imagine yourself performing a hobby, sport, or activity you often like to do. Your performance is getting smooth and is moving toward flawless play. There are no distractions; only you and the activity are in your mental scene. You are getting so good at the activity that it begins to produce a significant second income.

These are only two of the infinite number of daydreams you can have. Take a few moments each day to daydream. Focus your daydreams on important aspects of your life. Try to determine if the problems you normally encounter in these areas of your life are more easily solved as your daydreams help you leap the hurdles of disciplined thought.

CHECK YOUR PROGRESS

As historian Daniel Boorstin once said, "The main obstacle to progress is not ignorance, but the illusion of knowledge."[8] Many of the problems below hint at a knowledge that is illusory. Try not to be fooled into proceeding down the paths of normal knowledge. Instead, let the child inside rule your thoughts. Use your newfound flexibility to "play" with the problems. Your creative insight about the solutions will often come in a flash while your mind is exploring the possibilities.

PROGRESS PUZZLE 9.1

If a brick weighs 5 pounds and half a brick, what is the weight of a brick and a half?

PROGRESS PUZZLE 9.2

If it takes 4 men 6 hours to dig 8 holes, how long does it take one man to dig half a hole?

PROGRESS PUZZLE 9.3

If it takes 3 minutes to boil one egg, how long does it take to boil 3 eggs?

PROGRESS PUZZLE 9.4

How many times can you subtract the number 3 from the number 38?

PROGRESS PUZZLE 9.5

What is the next letter in this array of letters?

$$O$$
$$O\ T$$
$$O\ T\ T$$
$$O\ T\ T\ F$$
$$O\ T\ T\ F\ F$$
$$O\ T\ T\ F\ F\ S$$
$$O\ T\ T\ F\ F\ S\ S$$
$$O\ T\ T\ F\ F\ S\ S\ \underline{\quad}$$

PROGRESS PUZZLE 9.6

Bob has 6 pairs of brown socks and 8 pairs of blue socks in his drawer. What is the minimum number of loose socks he would need to remove to get a matched pair if he had to retrieve socks at night when he could not see the colors?

PROGRESS PUZZLE 9.7

A man who does not like to buy cigarettes makes his own from cigarette ends he collects. Six ends will make a cigarette. He has collected 31 ends. How many cigarettes can he make from these?

PROGRESS PUZZLE 9.8

Two joggers, initially 10 miles apart, start at the same instant toward each other along a straight road, each at a speed of 5 miles per hour. At the same instant a fly on the forehead of one of the joggers starts to fly at 12 miles per hour directly toward the other, lands on her forehead, and then continues to fly back and forth until they meet. Assuming the fly had no landing time, flies at a constant speed, and is squashed when the joggers collide, how far has it flown?

PROGRESS PUZZLE 9.9

A family consisting of a father, mother, and daughter decide to go on a picnic. They leave their house and head south for 1 mile. Before they can open the picnic basket, the daughter spies Papa bear. They decide to leave before the bear gives them any trouble. They walk east for 1 mile. Before they can open their picnic basket, the daughter spies Mama bear. They all decide that since too many bears are out today, they had best go home. They walk the mile north back to their house where they find that a bear—it must have been Baby bear—has ransacked their house.

What color was the bear who ransacked their house?

PROGRESS PUZZLE 9.10

How can you arrange 4 pennies in 2 straight lines with 3 pennies on each line?

Answers

9.1 Fifteen pounds. Each half brick weighs five pounds.

9.2 A person cannot dig half a hole.

9.3 Three minutes.

9.4 Once. Then you no longer have the number 38. Another creative answer is an infinite number of times. You can always subtract the number 3 from the number 38.

9.5 E. Each letter is the first in the spelling of the numbers: *One*, *Two*, *Three*, *Four*, et cetera.

9.6 Three socks. This is the minimum no matter how many socks of two colors he has in his drawer.

9.7 Six cigarettes. He makes 5 at first. With the ends from these 5 plus the 1 left over initially, he can make 1 more.

9.8 Twelve miles. The joggers cover the distance between them at a combined rate of 10 miles per hour. Since that initial distance was ten miles, they walk for one hour. The fly who is flying at twelve miles per hour covers twelve miles during that time.

9.9 White. It was a polar bear. The only way the family could have covered those distances in those directions was for their house to have been located at the north pole.

9.10 Arrange three coins in a triangle and put the fourth on top of one of them. Who ever said you had to restrict your problem solving to two dimensions?

Creativity is something that should give you pleasure rather than test anxiety. Fortunately, you can feel your creative abilities changing even if you do not test them per se. There are many examples: You can see how little time it takes for you to make up limericks or fall into a productive daydream. When you have a problem to solve, you can see how flexible your mind is at providing a range of possible solutions. You can also determine how quick you are on the uptake to a joke, and perhaps your own sense of humor and punning will improve.

An important factor in checking your creative progress, as with any form of progress, is to keep a record of it. A creative diary is a wonderful thing to look back on to see how far you have come or to examine when you are discouraged about your present rate of progress. In it you should record your limericks and the time it takes to produce them. You should record your daydreams. And most importantly, you should record the ideas or solutions that you have marshaled to solve problems. Examine each solution for its problem-solving heuristic: See whether you generalized or specialized the problem, whether you made an analogy, or whether the idea simply popped into your head before you began to list the alternatives.

Remember that your creative diary is a record of your creative progress and is thus a document every bit as important as your school record or resume. You should treat it with the respect any important document deserves.

PART THREE

Brain Exercise Regimens

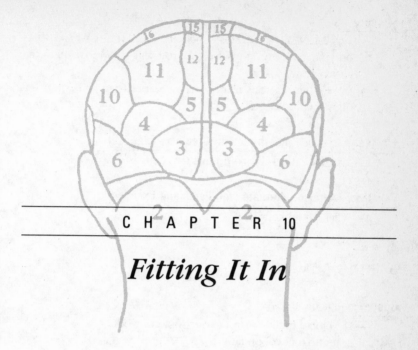

C H A P T E R 10

Fitting It In

This brain exercise routine is for those of you who have a jam-packed daily schedule and would like to improve your brain power during those in-between moments. Remember that the following routine is a sample. Feel free to substitute your preferred exercises as long as you tap the different brain functions.

AFTER BREAKFAST BUT BEFORE LEAVING FOR WORK

Spatial Exercise

—Feature calisthenics—imagine shapes and objects and rotate them in your mind's eye.

—Furniture arrangement in a mental room—imagine a room and mentally remove and rearrange the furniture.

Memory Exercise
—Peg list of daily activities—mentally hang your daily activities on your memory "pegs" so that you will remember them the entire day.
—Remember ten facts from morning paper (peg or home locations method).

Language Exercise (alternate with Creativity Exercise)
—Articulation aerobics—do five tongue twisters.

Creativity Exercise (alternate with Language Exercise)
—What would happen if . . .

DURING COMMUTE

Spatial mapping
—Develop a mental map of your route to work.
—Listen to a novel on tape.
—Vocabulympics—choose a target word and see how many words can be made from it.

DURING MEETINGS
—Doodling.
—Face-vase drawing.

DURING SHORT (FIVE-MINUTE) BREAKS FROM WORK ACTIVITY (You should perform two of these in the morning and two in the afternoon.)
—Jigsaw puzzle.
—Video game.
—Ambiguous meanings—make up sentences that have two meanings (e.g., "Flying planes can be dangerous.").
—DeBono's Plus, Minus, and Interesting—pick an issue and list the pluses, minuses, and interesting points about it.
—Inkblot interpretations—give all the associations an inkblot makes you think of. (You can also do this with clouds.)

—Alternatives—start with an image of a strange scene and provide a list of "explanations" for it.

—Limerick sense—make up two limericks.

AFTER DINNER AND BEFORE NIGHTTIME ACTIVITY (choose 1)

—Do the daily crossword puzzle.

—Read several pages from a novel.

—Analyze logic fallacies from day's activities—see how many examples of overgeneralizing, personal attacks, bad analogies, and circular arguments, etc., you can find.

—Plot a murder mystery—start with an image of the murder scene. Think of the relationships of the deceased. Then provide "explanations" for whether or not these significant others killed the victim.

RIGHT BEFORE BED (choose 1)

—Interpret an inkblot.

—Create an image—draw a random series of lines and shapes and create a picture from them.

—Analyze surface and deep structure from sentences in a novel.

—Play a video game.

WORKING TOGETHER

Having someone participate with you on a project can provide a big boost to your own efforts, and it can often make the project more enjoyable. The following brain exercises are meant to be performed with two or more participants.

SPATIAL
Mirrors

This is an old actor's exercise that allows you to communicate with someone in purely spatial terms. Stand in a relaxed position facing your partner. Take turns as the "mirror" partner. The mirror partner simply copies all the body movements of the other person as they might be seen in a mirror.

With three or more people, this can be an effective party game. The object of the audience participants is to guess which of the two mirror participants is the "mirror" and which is the initiator. As you develop your spatial skills with this exercise, it should become harder and harder for the audience to tell the initiator from the mirror partner.

Video Games

Any time you play against a competitor, you sharpen your skills. By playing Nintendo, or any other video game, against a partner, you begin to exercise your visuospatial abilities to their fullest. Besides, it is so much fun, you won't even think you are exercising.

Sprouts (see p. 87)

This is a nice game for exercising both spatial and logic functions. Start with three or four dots on a sheet of paper. Each player takes turns making a "move." A move consists of drawing a line that joins one dot to another dot or to itself (by closing back a loop). After the line is drawn, a new dot is placed anywhere along the line. But, there are two rules: (1) A line cannot cross itself or a previously drawn line, and it cannot pass through a previously made dot, and (2) no dot may have more than three lines growing out of it. You can play by having either the winner or the loser as the last one to make a move.

LANGUAGE

Tongue Twisters

Each player should make up a tongue twister. The partner has to say it 5 times, as fast as possible. The first player to stumble over the twister loses. For more than 2 players, make up a twister for the player to your left.

Find Words (2 players)

Each player has a word in mind composed of 4 or more letters, and each player states the number of letters in the word. Players alternately call out a word to guess the other player's word, and the other player tells the guesser how many letters match the word she has in mind. If, for example, I have in mind the word "mind," you might guess "mush." I would reply "one," for the one letter that matches. Then I would guess your word and you would tell me how many letters match. Then you might guess "milk," and I would reply "two." The game continues until one player guesses the word of the other.

Letters on the Go

Each player gets a letter of the alphabet and must use that letter to give a place and an activity. For example, the first player might say, "I'm going on a trip to Alcatraz, and I am going to Anchor Apple Arbors." The second player continues with the letter B, and might say something like. "I'm going on a trip to Brighton Beach, and I am going to Build Beautiful Barbershops.

Try variations on this game in which the activity has 4 words that all begin with the relevant letter, or—even harder—in which the activity relates directly to the place. Texas—Tell Tall Tales.

Scrabble

The oldies are often the best. (After all, they've withstood the test of time.) Scrabble is an excellent way to sharpen word recognition and generation abilities. And the effort to get the most points out of words really gets the adrenaline moving.

If you feel that you've reached a plateau with your game, you can always add on a few rules that increase the challenge. For example, you could set 4 or 5 as the minimum number of letters. Or, you could really spice up the game by limiting the words to adjectives or nouns.

MEMORY

Circle Numbers

A group of players form a circle facing each other. Each player takes a number and calls it out to the group. Then an object (e.g., a ball) is thrown from one player to another. Each player with the ball says his own number and that of the player to whom he is throwing. For example: "23 throws to 49." Any player who misses a number is out of the round. The last player who remains is the winner.

A Lot of Driving

The first player says, "I'm going on a trip, and I will drive to Austin." The next player says, "I'm going on a longer trip, and I will drive to Austin and Boston." The next player might say she's driving to Austin, Boston, and Charlotte. Players begin to drop out if they fail to remember one of the cities. The player who lasts the longest wins.

You can try a variation on this game by saying, "I am going on a trip, and in my suitcase I will pack Apples." The next player might say, ". . . and in my suitcase I will pack Apples and Books." Then: ". . . Apples, Books, and Cauliflower." The game goes on in the same way.

A clever way to bring word exercise into this memory game would be to modify each item on this list with an adjective that starts with the same letter. For example, I might be packing "Argentine Apples, Bank Books, and Chilled Cauliflower . . ."

LOGIC

Debate an Issue

This can be a most enlightening, but humbling, experience. Take a hot topic—abortion, capital punishment, environmental regulation, etc. Have two players take opposite sides of the issue—pro and con. (For fun, players can switch to the side opposing their normal beliefs.) The two debaters then take a few minutes to make up a list of 10 statements supporting or opposing the topic. Now the real exercise begins. Each player takes the other's list and tries to find logic fallacies in it— overgeneralizing, give-em-en-inch, personal attack, superstitious behavior, bad analogies, appeal to authority or crowds, circular arguments, and oversimplifying. The player who finds the most logic fallacies wins. (Of course, this will make you want to limit the fallacies in your own argument.)

What Would Happen If . . .

This is a twist on an old party game, and it could be in either the logic or creativity section—it's good for both. All players complete the question by thinking out the conjecture part. For example, what would happen if . . .

—Shakespeare had never been born?
—A cow jumped over the moon?
—The country's main tax computer broke down?
—An alien spaceship landed on the White House roof?

These are, of course, only a few of the infinite possibilites. Then, one player stands and gives a logical answer to her conjecture *without saying what it is*. For example, a player might say, "Television reception in the White House would be disrupted." Then, all the other participants have to guess what the conjecture was. If no participant guesses correctly (in this case, the alien spaceship on the White House is correct), then the first player gives another logical answer as a clue. The participant who guesses correctly gets to give the next clues for his conjecture.

CREATIVITY

Act a Story

Choose a simple story—a fairy tale or some other children's story will do. One player will be the actor, while another player is the narrator. The actor simply acts out the story as the narrator reads it.

A simple (and fun) variation on this game also challenges the creativity of the narrator. The actor defines herself to be a character standing in a place with an object. For example, the actor might say, "I am a *birdwatcher* standing in a *balloon factory*, and with me is an *umbrella*. The narrator makes up a short story using the character, place, and object while the actor acts it out. This can be a delightful party game if all participants trust each other not to pursue embarrassing or hostile stories.

Problem Solving

Each player states a problem without getting emotional about it. For example, a player might say, "I was given a tight deadline for a report. I made the deadline, but my boss didn't like the report. He asked a coworker to clean it up for me." All the other players now respond in turn by brainstorming about the problem. Each player simply states a (brief) solution to the problem. All players take turns, and players drop out when they no longer have a solution in mind. The last player (the one with the most solutions) has to give the next problem. Two rules: (1) The player with the problem has to be a "sponge"—has to soak it all up without saying anything and (2) no other player can assert that his solutions are superior. The idea is simply to generate as many solutions as possible.

Drawing Charades

This is a spatial creativity game. Variations on this game are currently quite popular. The idea is very much like charades. Instead of having to act out the meaning of a simple phrase while the other participants guess the words in it, you have to draw the phrase instead. The person who draws must remain silent while the other participants guess, and a time limit should be placed on the guessing.

SAMPLE BRAIN WORKOUT

This routine is for those of you who wish to exercise your brain systematically as an athlete would exercise various muscle groups. You should set up a brain workout space and keep regular brain fitness hours as if you were going to a fitness center to exercise your body.

For body workouts, instructors often ask that you alternate your attention to various muscle groups. This is so you do not fatigue any one group, thus preventing your workout from having its peak beneficial effect.

You will need to do the same thing with your brain workout. Since language and spatial functions involve the activity of left and right brain areas, respectively, an exercise regimen should take this into account by alternating work on language and spatial exercises.

Body fitness instructors also often ask that you keep a record of your performance. This is important for brain fitness exercises as well. Keep a brain workout diary. Record in it the time, error rate, or analyses of exercises we have discussed in previous chapters. With such a record, you will easily see the progression of your performance.

Alternate workouts A and B daily.

WORKOUT A	WORKOUT B
Language Functions	Spatial Functions
—vocabulympics (page 115) or daily crossword	—video game (page 208)
—read 10–20 pages of novel	—jigsaw puzzle
—analyze surface and deep structure of sentences in novel	—face-vase drawing
—practice a new language	—sketch a person's profile

Logic Functions

—logic fallacies from daily paper
  (letters to editor)
—deBono's Plus, Minus, Interesting (page 164)
—computer programming
—logic problems

Creativity Functions

—ink blots
—alternatives
—limerick sense
—punning
—daydreaming

Memory Functions

Memory exercises should be performed every day. Use peg words on the language days and chunking and locations on the spatial days. Increase the list of things you want to remember no more than twice a week. It is better to remember important things (e.g., shopping list) than trivial things (e.g., random words).

Language

—peg word method
  (page 148)

Spatial

—locations (page 145)
—chunking (page 150)
—tie faces to names
  (page 142)

Marathon Trainer

If in the near future you will be taking a difficult exam—e.g., an aptitude test or licensing exam—it would be helpful to add mental preparation to the specific preparation for the exam. A brain workout is no substitute for the real studying you may have to do, but it couldn't hurt as an adjunct method.

The following plan is for those of you familiar with the disciplined buildup of a protracted training period. It will also be useful as adjunct preparation for a difficult exam that is still several weeks away. Fifteen or twenty minutes is optimal for each exercise, and it is best not to take longer than thirty minutes for each. If the exam involves memorizing large amounts of material, you would do well to use the memory exercises on your material.

The workout follows the basic guidelines for marathon training. It has a buildup of intensity the first week, and it then alternates in intensity daily until a maximum intensity is attained on the third week. Rest periods are taken at the end of each week. The workout finally tapers off the last week to rest your brain in preparation for the exam. Those of you who would like a more protracted workout beyond the four weeks presented here can use the second and third week plans over and over until the final week before the exam. Then the fourth week plan should be used.

Also remember that sleep, enjoyment, physical exercise, and nutrition are important to maintain a basic level of brain conditioning. Try the brain exercise diet, and be sure to get twenty to thirty minutes of fun physical exercise three or four times a week. Keep in mind that any ballgame—tennis, racketball, basketball, etc.—provides excellent spatial exercise along with the physical exercise and eye-hand coordination.

WEEK 1: The Buildup
Day 1—solo Spatial (simple video game or face-vase drawing)
     solo Creativity (ink blots, clouds)
     solo Memory (locations or chunking)
Day 2—solo Language (e.g., vocabulympics)
     solo Memory (peg words)
Day 3—social Spatial (ballgame, mirrors)
Day 4—social Logic (What would happen if . . .)
Day 5—solo Spatial (jigsaw puzzle or sketch profile)
     solo Creativity (deBono's Plus, Minus, Interesting)
     solo Memory (chunking)
Day 6—social Language (letters on the go)
     social Memory (a lot of driving)
Day 7—take it easy and rest your brain

WEEK 2: A little more vigorous
Day 1—solo Spatial (face-vase and video game)
     solo Creativity (alternatives and daydreaming)
     solo Memory (locations)
Day 2—solo Language creativity (make up two limericks)
     solo Memory (peg words)

Day 3—solo Spatial (ballgame, competitive video game)

social Creativity (act a story)

social Memory (circle numbers)

Day 4—solo Language (crossword puzzle)

social Logic (debate an issue)

Day 5—solo Spatial (face-vase and video game)

solo Memory (chunking or locations)

Day 6—solo Logic (learning or practicing computer programming)

Day 7—take it easy or play one or two fun video games

WEEK 3: More vigorous; start
mixing hemisphere functions

Day 1—solo Spatial (sketch a profile, face-vase)

solo Creativity (puns and daydreams)

solo Memory (peg words)

Day 2—solo Language (crossword puzzle, read more than
normal)

social Logic (find fallacies)

solo Memory (chunking)

Day 3—social Spatial (competitive video game)

social Creativity (problem solving)

solo Memory (peg words)

Day 4—social Language (Scrabble)

solo Spatial (face-vase)

Day 5—social Creativity (problem solving)

social Memory (circle numbers, a lot of driving)

Day 6—social Logic (programming, what would happen
if . . .)

solo Spatial (sprouts)

Day 7—social Spatial (competitive video game)

WEEK 4: Even more vigorous;
then taper off near exam

Day 1—solo Language (crossword puzzle)

solo Logic (programming)

Day 2—social Spatial (ballgame or sprouts)
social or solo Creativity (drawing charades, day-dreaming)
solo Memory (chunking)
Day 3—social Language (vocabulympics)
solo Spatial (face-vase)
solo Logic (deBono's Plus, Minus, Interesting)
Day 4—social Spatial (ballgame or mirrors)
solo Language Creativity (puns and limericks)
solo Memory (locations)
Day 5—solo Logic (programming)
solo Spatial (video game)
Day 6—take your exam
Day 7—rest or play a video game

Long-Term Awareness Using Brain Diaries

Diaries are effective tools for tracking your progress and your feelings about that progress. They allow you to see where you've been, where you are now, and what trends you are making for the future. And it doesn't matter whether you are slipping in snatches of brain exercise in the midst of a busy schedule or performing a long-term disciplined brain workout. The record of your progress is the key to further development.

You may make copies of the diary page contained in this book, use a bound composition book or spiral notebook, or use a fancy sophisticated diary. It doesn't matter what you use as long as it is bound (looseleaf notebooks provide too much temptation to go back and alter the record), and a daily record can be made easily and efficiently.

To give you an idea of your outlook on the day, you might want to start with a test of mental speed or agility. You can use a timed test—a simple jigsaw or crossword puzzle—or a point-scoring test like those found in video games. Then you should write down your observations on your performance of each brain function. Finally, you should have enough room to write down any other observations you may have about the functioning of your brain. A sample diary entry appears on the following page:

Sample Brain Diary

11/8/90

Morning Outlook: Woke up this morning feeling a little tired—stayed up too late working on my report. But my jigsaw completion time was 4 min. 38 sec., a full four seconds less than my best time so far. My mental speed—at least for spatial functions—is pretty good this morning.

I felt better after drinking a cup of orange juice. Wonder what my jigsaw time would have been if I did it after breakfast. It's a spatial/creative day. Good sign.

Spatial—Sketched a profile and did a face-vase today. Getting coordinated on the copy side of the face-vase. Also played a Nintendo game at work, though Sharon caught me doing it. (But she doesn't care; she knows what I'm trying to do.) We had a presentation by our ad agency and I noticed I was picking up on their charts pretty quickly this morning.

Language—Not today, though I did read the morning paper fairly carefully.

Memory—Chunked ten items from morning paper. Still bouncing around in my head this evening, though I didn't think about them the rest of the day.

Logic—Not a logic day, but did notice Sharon oversimplifying, and John gave a circular argument, something about money to fight drug dealers.

Creativity—Had a problem to solve about a client today. Thought about it by specializing the issue and ferreting out analogies. Came up with the right idea. At least Sharon likes it.

Other Notes: Though I was working well today, I still felt sleepy. Had pasta for lunch—big mistake. About 1:30 P.M. I could hardly keep my eyes open. Should moderate next time I feel this way. Played Nintendo game with my son this evening, and he only beat me by ten points. He was impressed I did so well.

Your Own Brain Diary

Date: _____

Morning Outlook:

Spatial—

Language—

Memory—

Logic—

Creativity—

Other Notes:

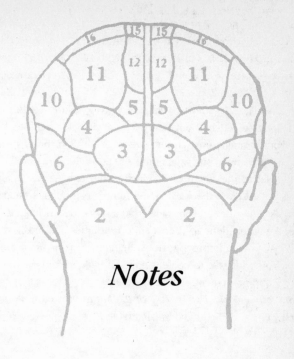

Notes

Chapter 1

1. For an entertaining and highly informative explication of the older ideas on brain size and intelligence, see Stephen Jay Gould's *The Mismeasure of Man*, New York: Norton, 1981.

2. Gleitman, H. *Psychology*, New York: Norton, 1981.

3. See William Angoff's discussion of the nature-nurture debate in *American Psychologist*, 43, 1988, 713–720.

4. Howard Gardner in *Frames of Mind* (New York: Basic Books, 1985) has identified six kinds of intelligence, but that is only one way to classify brain functions. We probably will not really know how to classify until we develop an ordered scheme for brain functions much like chemists have for elements. This scheme would show us the hierarchy of behavioral units built into our brains, and it could help us understand how

other brain functions are affected when we alter one brain function with exercise. My own discussion of classification of brain functions can be found in *The Journal of Psychology*, 120, 1986, 121–135. Nevertheless, Gardner's scheme is useful for the present state of knowledge, and it guided my discussion.

5. See Rushdie's *The Satanic Verses*, New York: Viking, 1988, p. 281.

6. In talking so much about improvement, it is tempting to look at the horizon of brain research and see what kinds of brain measurement might be coming our way. Some scientists think that abilities can be measured in the speed of conduction through nerve circuits. Others think chemistry is the wave of the future. You might someday be able to walk into a brain center and have a blood test, urinalysis, and brain speed workup done to see what your abilities are and how quickly it will take you to improve various elements of your brain function. For now, you will have to content yourself with measuring your own behavioral improvement.

7. From Penfield, W. *The Mystery of the Mind*, Princeton: Princeton University Press, 1975, quoted in Gleitman's *Psychology*, New York: Norton, 1981.

Chapter 2

1. National Research Council, *Recommended Dietary Allowances*, 10th Ed., National Academy Press, Washington, DC, 1989.

2. Amino acids come in two mirror image molecular forms—L and D. Only the L form is biologically significant.

3. Burton, B. T. *Human Nutrition*, New York: McGraw-Hill, 1976.

4. Nestle, M. *Nutrition in Clinical Practice*, Greenbrae, CA: Jones Medical Publications, 1985.

5. For 12 days, Spiers gave his research subjects capsules containing the FDA's maximum allowable limit of the NutraSweet sweetener: aspartame. From a report by S. Rovner, "NutraSweet: The Debate Continues," which originally appeared in *The Washington Post* and was quoted in *The Times-Picayune* (New Orleans, LA) May 26, 1987.

6. For more information on Gold's work, see "Sweet Memories," in *American Scientist*, vol. 75, 1987, 151–155.

7. Richard and Judith Wurtman at M.I.T. are among the world's experts on choline. Their many published scientific papers on choline show how it is active in brain function.

8. See Judith Wurtman's book, *Managing Your Mind and Mood Through Food*, New York: Rawson & Assoc., 1986.

9. Faelten, S., *The Complete Book of Minerals for Health*, Emmaus, PA: Rodale Press, 1981.

10. Sandstead, H. H. Neurobiology of Zinc. In Frederickson, C. J. et al. (Eds), *The Neurobiology of Zinc*, Part B, New York: Liss, 1984, pp. 1–16.

11. New York: McGraw-Hill, 1976.

12. Wurtman, *Managing Your Mind*.

Additional Souces of Information:

Rombauer, I. S. & Becker, M. S., *The Joy of Cooking*, New York: Bobbs-Merrill Co., 1975.

Nutritive Value of American Foods, U.S. Department of Agriculture, Handbook #456, 1988.

Chapter 3 *

1. Information about drug effects on the brain can be found in Goodman and Gilman's *The Pharmacological Basis of Therapeutics*, New York: MacMillan, 1980. See also Julien, R. M., *A Primer of Drug Action*, San Francisco: Freeman, 1981.

2. Haut, J. S., B. E. Beckwith, T. V. Petros, and S. Russell, "Gender Differences in Retrieval from Long-Term Memory Following Acute Intoxication with Ethanol," *Physiology and Behavior* 45, 1989, 1161–1165.

3. From Perl, D. P., and A. R. Brody, "Alzheimer's Disease: X-Ray Spectrometric Evidence of Aluminum Accumulation in Neurofibrillary Tangle-Bearing Neurons," *Science* 208, 1980, 297–299.

4. Martyn, C. N., D. J. P. Barker, C. Osmond, E. C. Harris, J. A. Edwards, and R. F. Lacey, "Geographical Relation between Alzheimer's Disease and Aluminum in Drinking Water," *The Lancet* January 14, 1989, 59–62.

5. Information on toxic metals can be found in Faelton, S., *The Complete Book of Minerals for Health*, Emmaus, PA: Rodale Press, 1981.

Chapter 4

1. For more information on reinforcing memories through sleep, see the writing of Bernard Davis, *Perspectives in Biology and Medicine* 28, 1985, 457–464.

2. Thompson, M. J., and D. Harsha, "Our Rhythms Still Follow the African Sun," *Psychology Today* January 1984, 50–54.

3. Recall that the conversion of tryptophan to serotonin in the brain also helps to relax you and focus your mental activity during the day. The sleep-inducing effect of tryptophan is more effective at night. Your natural circadian rhythms help to determine what the effects of tryptophan will be.

4. See Csikszentmihalyi's *Beyond Boredom and Anxiety: The Experience of Play in Work and Games* (San Francisco: Jossey-Bass, 1975).

5. Isen, A. "Positive Affect Facilitates Creative Problem Solving," *Journal of Personality and Social Psychology* 52, 1987, 1122–1131.

6. New York: Bantam, 1973.

Chapter 5

1. Wurtz, R. H., M. E. Goldberg, and D. L. Robinson, "Brain Mechanisms of Visual Attention," *Scientific American 246*, 1982, 124–135.

2. For additional exercises of this variety, see Reid Daitzman's book, *Mental Jogging: 365 Games to Enjoy, to Stimulate the Imagination, to Increase Ability to Solve Problems and Puzzles*. NY: R. Marek Publishers, 1980.

3. Edwards, B., *Drawing on the Right Side of the Brain*, Los Angeles: J. P. Tarcher, 1979.

4. Additional games and puzzles that serve to test spatial abilities can be found in books by Howard Gardner (*Frames of Mind*, NY: Basic Books, 1985), James Fixx (*Games for the Superintelligent* and *More Games for the Superintelligent*, NY: Doubleday, 1988), E. R. Emmett (*Brain Puzzler's Delight*, NY: Emerson Books, 1978), Martin Gardner (*Mathematical Carnival*, NY: Knopf, 1975), and Gyles Brandreth (*Classic Puzzles*, NY: Harper & Row, 1986).

Chapter 6

1. For more discussion of poets and language, see *Frames of Mind*, by Howard Gardner (NY: Basic Books, 1985).

2. For a more detailed discussion of this phenomenon, see *Left Brain, Right Brain*, by S. Springer and G. Deutsch (NY: W. H. Freeman, 1985).

3. Goodglass, H., "Disorders of Naming Following Brain Injury," *American Scientist* 68, 1980, 647–655.

4. This is the theory of David Rumelhart and James McClelland, scientists at University of California at San Diego and Carnegie Mellon University,

respectively. Their theory can be found in *Mechanisms of Language Acquisition*, edited by B. MacWhinney (Hillsdale, NJ: L. Erlbaum Assoc., 1987).

5. For additional tongue twisters, see Schwartz, A., *A Twister of Twists; A Tangler of Tongues* (Philadelphia: Lippincott, 1972), Brandreth, G., *Word Games* (NY: Harper & Row, 1986), and Brandreth, G., *Joy of Lex* and *More Joy of Lex* (NY: Morrow, 1982). See also Dr. Seuss's *Fox in Socks* (NY: Beginner Books, 1965).

6. According to Donald Spence, in *Psycholinguistic Research*, edited by D. Aaronson and R. W. Rieber (Hillsdale, NJ: L. Erlbaum Assoc., 1979).

7. For a thorough preparation in the verbal martial arts, see S. H. Elgin's *The Gentle Art of Verbal Self-defense* (NY: Dorset Press, 1980).

8. And see Elgin, *Verbal Self-Defense*.

9. Tests #1 and #2 use words taken from lists found in *Spell It Right*, by Harry Shaw (Barnes & Noble, 1961) and *Resource Materials for Teachers of Spelling*, by Paul Anderson (Burgess, 1959). The "old" words were found in *The Critical Spelling Book*, by Solomon Lowe, 1755, reprinted in 1967 by Scolor Press, England.

Chapter 7

1. For more discussion of the Russian memory expert, see A. R. Luria's *The Mind of a Mnemonist* (NY: Basic Books, 1968).

2. See *Memory: Surprising New Insights into How We Remember and Why We Forget* (Reading, MA: Addison-Wesley, 1980), by Elizabeth Loftus.

3. Loftus, *Memory*.

4. From D. O. Hebb, "On Watching Myself Get Old," *Psychology Today* November 1978.

5. Loftus, *Memory*.

6. From research by Willard Rodgers and Regula Herzog of the Institute for Social Research at the University of Michigan. See *Journal of Gerontology* 42, 1987, 387–394.

7. From Rowe, J. W., and R. L. Kahn, "Human Aging: Usual and Successful," in *Science* 237, 1987, 143–149.

8. Hebb, "On Watching Myself Get Old."

9. Reason, James, and Klara Mycielska, *Absent-Minded? The Psychology of Mental Lapses and Everyday Errors* (Englewood Cliffs, NJ: Prentice-Hall, 1982).

10. From *Improve Your Memory Skills* (Englewood Cliffs, NJ: Prentice-Hall, 1982), by Francis Bellezza.
11. See Alan Baddeley's *Your Memory: A User's Guide* (NY: MacMillan, 1982).

Chapter 8

1. See Cohen, M., and E. Nagel in *An Introduction to Logic and the Scientific Method* (NY: Harcourt Brace, 1934), pp. 185–86.
2. From Stuart Chase's *Guides to Straight Thinking* (NY: Harper, 1956).
3. See Paul Rozin and April Fallon's article in *Psychology Today* July 1985, pp. 60–63.
4. From "A Proposed Mechanism of Emotion," by J. Papez, in *Archives of Neurology and Psychiatry* 38, 1937, 725–743.
5. From an article by Richard Nisbett and colleagues in *Science* vol. 238, 1987, 625–631.
6. See Edward deBono's *Thinking Course* (NY: Facts on File, 1985).
7. From *Life on the Mississippi*, by Mark Twain, quoted in Stuart Chase's *Guides to Straight Thinking* (NY: Harper, 1956).
8. For more detail on circular reasoning, also known as begging the question, see Robert Gula's book *Nonsense: How to Overcome It* (NY: Stein & Day, 1979). This example was suggested in different form by his book.
9. Additional logic exercises can be found in *Games for the Superintelligent* and *More Games for the Superintelligent*, by James Fixx (NY: Doubleday, 1972); *Mathematical Carnival*, by Martin Gardner (NY: Knopf, 1975); *Brain Puzzler's Delight*, by E. R. Emmet (NY: Emerson Books, 1978); and *To Mock a Mockingbird*, by Raymond Smullyan (NY: Knopf, 1985).
10. The first three logic problems are suggested from classics collected in Fixx's books cited above.

Chapter 9

1. See *The Act of Creation* (NY: Penguin, 1990), by Arthur Koestler.
2. See *Frames of Mind: The Theory of Multiple Intelligences* (NY: Basic Books, 1983), by Howard Gardner.
3. Sperry is quoted in *Left Brain, Right Brain* (NY: W. H. Freeman, 1981), by S. Springer and G. Deutsch.
4. For more discussion of these dichotomies, see Springer and Deutsch's *Left Brain, Right Brain*.

5. For additional creativity games, see *Creative Growth Games* (NY: Jove, 1977), by Eugene Raudsepp and Julia Hough; and Edward deBono's *Thinking Course* (NY: Facts on File, 1985).

6. See Raudsepp and Hough, *Creative Growth Games*.

7. Koestler, *Act of Creation*.

8. Boorstin, D. J. *The Discoverers: A History of Man's Search to Know His World and Himself* (NY: Random House, 1985).

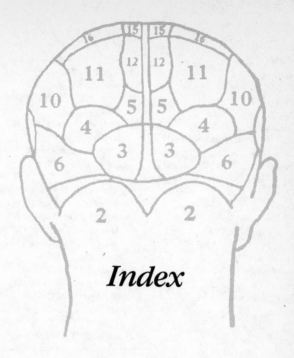

Index